IN THE TRACK OF SPEED

IN THE
TRACK OF SPEED

by

STIRLING MOSS

FREDERICK MULLER LIMITED

LONDON

FIRST PUBLISHED BY FREDERICK MULLER LTD
PRINTED IN GREAT BRITAIN BY
COX AND WYMAN LTD LONDON
FAKENHAM AND READING

CONTENTS

5

LIST OF ILLUSTRATIONS

ILLUSTRATIONS

Facing page

1

THE GATES CRASH OPEN

IT is said of those who are born to inherit a comforting share of this world's goods that they are born with silver spoons in their mouths; well, I might be said to have been born with a spanner in my mouth. My father, in his younger days, was a racing motorist, and my mother frequently competed in rallies and trials. So, as it were, there was a smell of petrol in my cradle and it is not really surprising that motor racing came to be my career.

Motor racing is quite different from all other sports, because success does not depend on the individual prowess of the expert.

Mere possession of a first-class set of clubs or tennis rackets does not make a man a champion golfer or tennis player, but Fangio himself can get nowhere unless the implement of his sport, i.e. the car, is superlatively good. It is equally true, of course, that the driver himself must possess those faculties which go to make the expert mile-eater. Don't ask me what the essential ingredients are, because I don't know. Theorists say we must have a perfect sense of balance, superb sight, abnormally quick reactions so that our brains signal to our muscles in the briefest space of time. We must have cool, calculating minds and physical dexterity. Personally, I prefer to regard the ability to drive fast cars a little faster than most people, as an intangible, almost abstract thing, like an ear for music, but with a motor car perhaps it's balance. It is something you cannot learn unless the fundamentals are inherent. But to retain your

9

prowess, there is one very prime essential; you must keep yourself absolutely fit.

A race driver may not be an athlete, but his life depends on physical fitness. To succeed, he must keep himself in strict training, avoid all excesses and concentrate on the job; although of course he need not think and dream about motor racing all the time; on the contrary, a certain amount of mental relaxation is necessary.

Obviously motor racing is dangerous, but its exponents do not run the risks that are so often supposed. Disaster results from the unexpected much more often than from any mistake on the part of the driver. As a result of practice, which must be thorough, he should know exactly what he can do. He should know the precise speed at which he can take a bend and he should know, to an inch, the most effective point for braking and for acceleration. It is, in fact, almost a routine job. Personally, I think practice is more dangerous than the race, as the driver does more experimenting.

One thing of which he may be certain, indeed *must* be certain, is that his car has been put into the highest state of preparedness for the task that is ahead of him. Expert mechanics have tuned it to perfection; the gear ratios have been adapted to the course and as far as it lies within the compass of human endeavour, the car on the starting line is what in horse-racing parlance would be called "trained to the minute". To say that nothing succeeds like success is very true. Those drivers who, by their prowess, have shown themselves to be in the top flight are more easily able to secure cars with real winning chances than those who are relatively of the rank and file of their profession.

Champion jockeys are in demand by the owners of race-horses with pretensions to winning classic races, and so, with motor racing, the man who has a string of successes behind him gets a better chance of joining a Grand Prix team than his less fortunate fellows. But if I am to digress, let me do so as and when the occasion is suitable, so that I can start telling this story chronologically.

When little more than a child, I sat on my father's lap behind the wheel of a car and he allowed me to steer. My fingers itched to do more, and I would sit up in the paternal lap full of pride. At the age of ten or eleven I became the owner of an elderly and decrepit little 7-h.p. car, which cost Dad £15 and probably a few heartaches. I was not old enough to drive on the roads, but there was plenty of room, and there were no restrictions about driving about our farm. There were lanes and pathways and fields, and before long I had planned a rough and ready circuit and spent hours driving round it in the little Austin. It was great fun, but it was also quite instructive, because I discovered some of the fundamentals of race driving in my keenness to get a few more "knots" out of the car. Dad seemed to alternate between discouraging and encouraging me. He taught me all he could—and that was plenty—he showed me how to "tune" and lighten the little car and those that followed it, and he took me in his own car on one or two trials, but at the same time he frowned on my avowed intention of becoming a racing driver.

Then the time came to take out a licence and drive on the public roads. In 1948 when I was eighteen, I overcame the resistance of my parents to a racing career and received enthusiastic support. About that time, too, John Cooper, who, like me, had a father who was keen on motoring and who, in fact, owned a garage at Surbiton, was building little 500 c.c. racing cars, equipped with motor-cycle engines. Certainly these were the speediest little cars available for the money I had to spend.

I recall that John Cooper built his prototype car with all sorts of odds and ends; in fact he used part of an air-raid shelter in the construction of the chassis. Dad and I haunted that garage while my car was being built! I must have been a devil of a nuisance as suggestions were made to modify and improve the power-weight ratio. At last the car was ready and delivery taken.

Where's the competitions calendar? What events were there to enter? Ah, Shelsley Walsh, famous for years as a classic hill climb. But no; nobody had heard of Stirling Moss. My entry was not accepted, and my soaring spirits were damped. But not for long. I entered for the Prescott Hill climb, another famous event, and this was accepted. The domestic atmosphere changed immediately. From amiable tolerance of my obsession, my parents stood 100 per cent behind me. It was as though they had said: "Right, son, you've beaten down our opposition; let's all see what can be done."

I had not driven my Cooper more than a few miles when, packing it into an adapted horse-box, I set off for Prescott.

There I was on the starting line, ready and eager, confident, yet nervous and determined. We were allowed two runs, and on the first of these I did not record a particularly good time. Being my first competition run I was undoubtedly a little over-anxious; but I had marked the peculiarities of the hill and hoped that my second run would be faster. It was. The Cooper shot off the line beautifully, the hill lost many of its terrors and I was up and over in the fastest time ever recorded in the 500 c.c. class. That was a grand start to my career. The record was of very short duration, faster times being recorded by three other competitors, but I was placed fourth and I had temporarily placed a record to my credit.

A month later, I competed in the Brighton and Hove Club's hill climb at Stanmer Park. Competing against me was Eric Brandon, who had not only given me some wise advice before Prescott, but had stolen my record from me. I put up quite a difficult target with a first-time climb of slightly under a minute, and up went Eric to lower it by a fraction. But that was his second run, and I had mine to come, which is always a nice feeling. I went up that hill like a man possessed, and clipped off something under half a second from Eric's time. I had won my first motor-racing trophy, and the tally was very satisfying. First event, record time; second event, the winner.

Another month elapsed, and I took my baptism in circuit racing, as distinct from hill climbs, on the Brough airfield. It poured in torrents during the race, which was run in two heats and a final. With a win in the heat and the same in the final, I put my first racing success in the bag. There was an eight-lap handicap to follow, and I felt it quite an honour to be the backmarker, running into third place after a lap, first place after three laps and managing to hold my position to the end.

In the autumn I made my first appearance at Goodwood. This was something different; a big meeting held by the British Automobile Racing Club and a big crowd of knowledgeable critics there. I think I rather surprised myself by putting up a fast practice lap. I won the race at 71·92 miles an hour, and also put up the fastest lap. That meant a nice little cheque for twenty guineas as prize money and also the rather heady wine of being sought by the Press photographers. A few more minor successes, and the year finished with the very gratifying analysis of eleven wins in the fifteen events in which I had competed. It cost me a little more than I had earned in prize money and trophies, but the balance was on my side, for I had gained some valuable experience and had already made something of a reputation. I must explain here that in the "old days" it was far easier to be successful, as there were far fewer competitors.

Next year we would go out for bigger game, but the opening gambit gave me my biggest disappointment so far. I had sold my Cooper and bought another one, with an alternative 1,000 c.c. Jap V twin engine. In the first event, with the 500 c.c. engine, I was out of the hunt on the first lap with a broken piston, so I changed over to the bigger power unit and opened the year's account by winning the Easter Handicap at nearly 80 miles an hour.

It is time, I think, for me to say that I have no intention of writing a factual compendium of race results, but to describe the highlights of drama which must come to all of us who, crowding the miles into minutes, engage in contests which call for split-second decisions. So far I have tabulated my first year's racing with the sole intention of showing you the good fortune which attended my early efforts. But I was still lacking in experience, still a long way from the vanguard of race drivers. I was, in fact, a pupil who had done rather well in his elementary lessons and had, as it were, qualified for secondary school.

For a period I carried on with my "double-barrelled" car with its optional 500 c.c. and 1,000 c.c. engines, and my run of luck continued, with a nice little piece of encouragement when I won the curtain-raiser in the form of a 500 c.c. race at the First British Grand Prix meeting at Silverstone. Then came my first road race, as distinct from hill climbs and aerodrome peripheries. I had been elected a member of the British Racing Drivers' Club which, I remember, was a great honour for me, and I entered for the Manx Cup race in the Isle of Man, which was a sort of "round-the-houses" contest in the environs of Douglas. Quite a thrill when I found myself at the head of the field after one circuit, and an even greater one when the end of the second lap produced for me a commanding lead of half a minute. Then the engine went dead and there I was, sitting impotently behind the wheel while car after car passed me. That is part of the racing game. The engine seems to be singing a glorious song of victory and then, all of a sudden, its voice is choked and you are out of the hunt. But in the course of time you get used to these inevitable occurrences and take them with philosophical forbearance.

My next venture saw me "blooded" in the exciting, dramatic pursuit of Continental racing. The scene of my baptism was at Lake Garda, that lovely spot in Italy, and I drove there rather jubilantly because I had been offered and had accepted £50 starting money. It was, of course, very acceptable, but more so was the realisation of the fact that race promoters had come to consider that I was worth subsidising as a starter. When I reached Italy I discovered that the motor-racing atmosphere was different from that which I knew in England. There was nothing lukewarm about the enthusiasm. Motor racing was a major sport, and the national heroes were such men as Tazio Nuvolari, Guiseppe Farina and Alberto Ascari. Everywhere you went the talk was of racing cars and racing men.

In this fervent, excited atmosphere I was a clown. They laughed at my Cooper which, it must be confessed, did not measure up in dignity and impressiveness to those lovely thoroughbreds of Italy and France. They had never seen a racing car like it before, and to them it was a joke. Their smiles turned to curiosity as I took up position on the starting line and to astonishment when, after the first lap, they saw me tucked in nicely behind the great Villoresi and Tadini on their much-loved Ferraris, occupying third place and well ahead of any of my competitors in the 1,100 c.c. class. The excitement of the chase, thank goodness, obliterated from my mind the horrible spectacle which confronted me soon after the start.

Count Sterzi, a dashing driver, had overshot a turn, crashed into a pylon and toppled over a cliff-like bank. As I recall the incident now, it seems to me that I shook myself like a retriever coming out of the water to get the shock of it out of my system. Passing the stands I noticed my father gesticulating wildly, calling on me to slow down a bit. Why? Was something wrong? Could he see a fault in the car which had not come to my notice? Then I realised that he was trying to pass on the cautionary message which all good managers and pit bosses send when the position warrants it. He wanted me to "save my horses"

15

because I was well in the lead in my class. Throughout that race of nearly 100 miles I pretty well kept the two Ferraris in sight and finished third; but it was only a heat.

In the final I again chased the two Ferraris round the course, running away from my class opponents, beating the record for the course and landing a nice £200 prize. What an ovation I got. The jeers became cheers. Press photographers crowded round me and the car; my father became a rejuvenated youngster, with a most delightful exhibition of boyish enthusiasm.

...eath at Goodwood, August 1950, the first season Stirling drove for H.W.M. (*Photo: Guy Griffiths*)

...miserable weather. The two cars immediately behind Stirling Moss ...rt of the very successful Simca Gordini team.

(*Above*): Stirling with his very first racing car, the Cooper J.A.P., and his sister Pat. (*Photo: Graphic*)

(*Below*): Stirling at the Tring home of his parents with Judy, his alsatian. (*Photo: Hulton Press Ltd.*)

(*Above*): A superb shot of Stirling in a four-wheel drift with the Cooper Norton 500 c.c. car at Silverstone. It was in this formula and this type of car that Stirling made his first appearance and climbed the first rung of the ladder of his career. (*Photo: N. W. Norman*)

(*Below*): With Mum and Dad after winning the 500 c.c. race at Silverstone, August 1950. (*Photo: T. D. Rowe*)

(*Above*): An unusual shot of the "C that Stirling achieved his first majo the same eve

(*Below*): A busy scene in the smal whom Stirling obtained much of

(*Above*): With the late John F

(*Below*): With the H.W.M. in were pa

2

TRICKS OF THE TRADE

I

HIGH praise is a tonic, but it can also be intoxicating. I was still in my teens, and I must say that I revelled in the tributes paid me by eminent motoring correspondents. It was about this time that Basil Cardew published in the *Daily Express* an interview with the great Tazio Nuvolari, then the acknowledged maestro of them all. During this interview Mr. Cardew reported him as saying: "Watch Stirling Moss; he is going to be one of the great drivers of the world."

How did this affect me? Well, as I read it I glowed with delight, but I knew that I had a lot to learn and a long way to go. My successes had been achieved on a type of car which had brought motor racing within the financial scope of the amateur enthusiast, but I had had no experience of the powerful, superb Grand Prix cars. I was still a fledgling, and knew nothing of the real technique of motor racing outside those events confined to what were known as the *voitures des petites cylindres*. I had some faith in myself, but it was good to know that others also had faith in me.

Gone entirely was any parental opposition to my chosen career, and I think that my father's chief interest in life had come to be the exploits of his son.

Shortly before my twentieth birthday I was invited to compete in the small car race at the Rheims Grand Prix meeting. The invitation paid high dividends on my success at Lake Garda, for I was offered the very considerable amount of

17

£200 as starting money. Really, things began to take on a very rosy hue. I was getting into the big money. I am afraid I did not earn that very nice little sum, because after putting up a rather remarkable speed of 140 m.p.h. on my 1,000 c.c. Cooper and seeming to be going well, the driving chain broke when I was nearly a mile from home. It was a very hot day, but it was my job to finish somehow and I pushed that broken-down car for what seemed very much more than a mile and was officially placed eighth. But that meeting at Rheims stands as a landmark in my career, for I tried for the first time the art of slip-streaming. This means getting a kind of tow from the car in front.

What you do is to tuck in behind a faster car, so that you are more or less sucked along in the "partial vacuum"* caused by the pacemaker's car. It is a fairly hazardous proceeding, because to get the full benefit of the tow you have to close in to a mere two or three yards from the car in front, and to do that when you are travelling at probably up to 180 miles an hour in Sports and Grand Prix cars means that the slightest error of judgment by the man who is inadvertently and perhaps rather crossly helping you along may mean involving you in an accident. But it really is an enormous advantage. You can travel faster on less power, and so save your engine while maintaining a better than standard speed.

If you can get a "lift" this way for mile after mile, you can then seek an opportunity with your "rested" engine to slip by the pacemaker, grab the lead and hold it. Obviously it is most effective if you are competing in a class event and can get behind one of the fast competitors in a more powerful class.

One of the most remarkable instances of aerodynamics occurred when John Cobb went for the land speed record

---

* A car travelling through the atmosphere at speed, leaves in its wake an area of low pressure, created by air flow currents due to the parting of the air layer. A car travelling behind in very close proximity enjoys the advantage of decreased air or wind resistance.

on the Salt Flats of Utah in 1938. The designer of that car was the very eminent Reid Railton. Standing beside Reid Railton during a practice run was Laurence Cade who, as motoring correspondent of *The Star*, was reporting the record attempt for his paper. When the run was over Railton said to him: "Let's go and look at the car. I want to see if there are any dents in the back." There were—dents caused by the back lash of air which acted as a pusher to the record breaker.

I don't suppose my slip-streaming at Rheims was very effective, though it taught me enough to know that, with practice, it could most definitely be used as a way of getting the equivalent of more horses under the bonnet than the designers put there. Since then, of course, I have used it as and when occasion offers, but you can bet your bottom dollar that I choose my pacemaker. He has to be a tip-top driver. A corollary to slip-streaming is the art of preventing other drivers from using you in the same way.

I remember an occasion when, in a Grand Prix race at Monza, I was getting a tow from Maurice Trintignant and my speed was getting a bonus of 15 m.p.h. over its normal maximum. Up came Simon, a team mate of Trintignant, and tried to get on to my tail. As I have said, you have to be pretty careful when you are indulging in this business, so I thought I would make things a little uncomfortable for the young Frenchman. I began to juggle with the wheel as though I were in trouble. My car, responding to the wheel, began to take an unsteady course, and the bluff worked. Simon thought there must be something wrong with my steering; he dropped back instead of occupying the hazardous slip-stream zone, and I was able to get into Trintignant's stream again and carry on with the magnet-like suction aid.

It was only a few days after my failure at Rheims that I fulfilled an engagement at Zandvoort, the classic Dutch course. It was here that I experienced my first introduction to the extraneous risks that we have to run. I shot off the starting line like a bullet out of a gun in the 500 c.c. race and, as I did so, the mechanic of another car stepped back across the road in front of me and escaped with his life by about a millimetre. There is now a very excellent rule which compels the mechanics to leave the track as soon as the minute alarm has sounded.

I won my race at Zandvoort all right, but I won something much more important. I saw a man motor racing as though he were reclining comfortably in an armchair, almost nonchalantly. Nothing tense, just a picture of relaxation and ease. He sat well back in the cockpit with his arms almost outstretched as they held the wheel. I watched him go round the circuit and I don't think I would have been very surprised if he had lit a cigar and started smoking it contentedly at his two- or three-miles-a-minute gait. I stood enthralled; I felt like a débutante at a fashion show, for here was a style that I had never seen before. I "bought the model"; that is to say I was so profoundly impressed that I decided that here was a famous driver on whom I would model my own style. I did so, and to this very day I feel that my first sight of Dr. Guiseppe Farina influenced my formative years as a racing motorist more than anything else. Since then, my comfortable driving position has been commented upon by critics and I can tell you that I owe it to the ex-world champion Farina. I suppose the influence of the old masters is apparent in the achievements of the moderns in other branches of life.

Later, I was to do a little hero-worshipping of another very great driver, but at that time I regarded Farina as the very epitome of all that I hoped to become. I saw Farina very soon afterwards among a veritable galaxy of Continental stars in the International race at Silverstone. I dearly wanted a mount in the newly promoted sports car race, and cast longing eyes at the Jaguars. But nobody seemed to want me. I might have done some excellent things on "the small fry", but that wasn't to say that I would be any good with bags of power under the bonnet. In any case, sports car racing was an entirely different proposition from the "nursery" lobs in the 500 c.c. or even 1,000 c.c. classes. That is more or less what I was given to understand, so having been pipped by Eric Brandon, my first of all tutors, in the 500 c.c. race, I assumed the rôle of spectator and registered a little more admiration for Farina.

One or two minor successes, and we came to the end of 1949, on which I was able to look back with a great deal of satisfaction.

I said good-bye to my Cooper, because John Heath had invited me to join his team of H.W.M. drivers, so that now I was a fully-fledged professional jockey and not a mere free-lance running his own horses. Most of 1950 was spent in Continental engagements aboard the H.W.M. whose valiant challenges were overwhelmed by the far greater power of the European cars. We experienced fun and games at Naples in July, though it finished for me on the "blood wagon", a satirical name given to the ambulance.

The start of the trouble lay with a rather selfish driver who shall be nameless, who refused to allow me to pass. As I got into position to do so he edged out to stop me. This went on for quite a while when Lance Macklin caught us up and, seeing the stubborn driver ahead of me pull out for another baulk, began his dash through on the inside. The obstructor swerved in to prevent him, and I seized the opportunity of shooting by on the outside. A little later I became involved in an accident because of the very much more sporting behaviour of another driver. I had just rounded a bend and was ready to pass another driver on the ensuing curve. He drew over to allow me to pass, but the tail of his car swung out, hit one of my front wheels, burst a tyre and sent me spinning round in the track at around 85 miles an hour. I finished up practically in a tree, broke my knee and knocked out several teeth. I must have been practically

21

unconscious, but my subconscious apparently operated and I ran away from danger for a few yards and then collapsed.

It is a curious psychological phenomenon that when you are ill, either as a result of an accident or from some malady, you always feel a little foolish. Although I was naturally in some pain after that crash, I was more disturbed mentally than physically. Hospital beds make me feel so completely incapable. Instead of being an entity, you are a mere patient, something less than a man who must be patched up and coddled and nursed while, most ungenerously, you are thinking to yourself: "When can I get out of this place?" Well, it was not long before I was discharged with one leg in plaster of Paris, but otherwise O.K.; though I am quite sure that my sojourn in hospital was lessened by my own impatience.

II

In less than a fortnight, much against everybody's advice, I was at the wheel again. I had returned to England and decided that I would have a go for an Open Challenge Trophy race at Brands Hatch. I couldn't walk very well, because my leg was still in its plaster, but that didn't seem to me any reason why I shouldn't drive. I recall how dozens of people came up to me in the paddock and told me I was barmy, crazy, idiotic and all the other synonyms there are for being mentally unbalanced. The doctor had told me that if I damaged my knee again I would have to have a metal plate in it, and I rather rudely rejected his advice to rest for a while by telling him that the next time it might not be my knee but my neck. It happened to be neither, for after winning my heat in the Trophy event I had to drop out of the final with engine failure.

My leg was still stiff when the Silverstone International meeting came round again, but I had started off well in the curtain-raiser with a new Norton-engined Cooper. The field left me at the start because of a seized clutch, and I had to be push-started; but my car had the legs, or should I say the wheels of the others, and after being last away I managed to head them all off in the second lap to win by twelve seconds. The Formula 1 (Grand Prix type) race followed and I drove an H.W.M., but the car just wasn't fast enough and I had to be content with sixth place. However, the day ended on a pleasant note.

You will recall that I had been a little sad and peeved at the Silverstone International meeting the year before because nobody seemed to think I was good enough to be entrusted with a high-powered car in the sports car event. Had I won my spurs by now, or was it that Tommy Wisdom considered that this was so? Because Tommy came to me and asked if I would like to drive his XK120 in the Tourist Trophy race the following September. Would I not! I could have hugged Tommy for his faith in me, and I accepted on the spot. The British Tourist Trophy event is one of the most classical and certainly the richest in tradition, of any race on the international calendar.

It was first promoted in the morning of motoring time, and among its winners are some of the greatest names in the game; men among the pioneers like J. S. Napier, the Hon. C. S. Rolls, founder of the great Rolls-Royce firm, Sir Algernon Lee Guinness and his brother Kenelm. Later winners were Kaye Don, the superb German driver Rudolf Caracciola, maestro of them all Tazio Nuvolari, and Freddie Dixon. What a gallant and famous company with whom to be associated in the annals of motor racing! Here were names which were the heroes of my youth, names I revered. To be given a chance of driving in the T.T. would have appealed to anyone in that embryonic stage of his career that I was in.

The great day dawned in the autumn of 1950, a day to damp the ardour of the most enthusiastic. A gale howled across the course, bringing with it torrential rain. The howling of the wind, like the wail of a banshee; the bending trees threatening to blow down on the course, the collapse of the Press tent, torn down by the fury of the elements; what a day for racing! Would they abandon the race? No: we were off in good time, with all the cars throwing up a watery wake so as to give the impression that it was a race between motor boats rather than cars. Conditions on the course were appalling; visibility was reduced owing to the twilight which was all that filtered down from the darkened sky.

Before I had completed half a lap I, in common with every other driver, was soaked, but the car behaved beautifully. It gave me far fewer anxious moments than I had anticipated, but my chance of winning seemed more and more remote as I went on. After the first circuit I was second; comforting in a way, but I felt that I could not possibly drive any faster. I chased the leader round on the second lap and eventually I was able to pass him and held premier position. With two hours' racing behind me I had the advantage of two minutes, which is quite a lot, but I could not ease up; my rivals might be keeping something up their sleeves.

Things became easier; the serenity of confidence had settled on me and the hazards became less formidable. I knew roughly what speed I could take the corners without in any way jeopardising the stability of the car. Its engine, never faltering, was singing to me as I occasionally took a mouthful of torrential rain. As the goal drew nearer, so my spirits rose until all my doubts were settled in that sublime feeling of utter confidence that at times comes to a man. So, I presume, do our athletes, our Bannisters and Chataways feel when the mighty urge of their final sprint takes them to leadership at the tape.

There were no risks; the corners flashed up at me and were gone. The last lap arrived and the car was going as well as ever, but the hounds were in hot pursuit; I must shake them off. In that last glorious circuit, which I shall ever remember, I set up a new record for the course at 77 miles an hour, and the sweet music of the crowd's plaudits, the lovely sight of the chequered flag, told me that I had joined the ranks of the old masters.

Prize money and bonuses netted me a very satisfactory increase to my bank account; but, believe me, it counted for practically nothing compared with the delight at having won the classic Tourist Trophy. Tommy Wisdom had given me my chance, and I had made the most of it. Certainly I had never driven better than on that gale-ridden day on the Dundrod course, and whatever fate may have in store for me I do not think I shall ever be better rewarded. Indeed, as I look back on it, I sometimes think that, in spite of my confidence, perhaps because of it, I was a little reckless, having regard to the appalling conditions; but if fortune favours the brave, no doubt it does the same, now and again, for the reckless.

From my victory stemmed official recognition for, some time later, I was to become No. 1 driver in the official Jaguar team. It paid off another dividend, for after Leslie Johnson and I had demonstrated the qualities of the XK120 by averaging over 107 miles an hour for twenty-four hours on the Montlhery track in France, I was awarded the Gold Star of the British Racing Drivers' Club and the Richard Seaman Trophy for the best overseas performance of the year. Success had come to me, but not much money, for although my gross earnings for the year were £5,500, my credit balance at the bank showed a mere £700 after expenses. Motor racing is an expensive business, but at any rate I had made a profit and may be said to have finished my apprenticeship and passed out with honours. Now I had to get more experience and study the other sides of motor racing.

Towards the end of the year, there was a 1,000 miles rally promoted by the *Daily Express*. I drove an Aston Martin in company with Lance Macklin, and we had a lot of fun. We were, in fact, rather naughty, because both of us agreed that instead of conforming to a set average speed in accordance with the official schedule, we would really bat along and see how much sleep we could get at the various control centres. We were doing well and had quite a comfortable time of it until we got to the steep and winding Bwlch-Y-Gross, which at one time was regarded as an almost unclimbable test hill. The way was barred by a great crocodile of stationary cars. I looked quizzically at Lance and he winked back at me, so we took the outside of the stream with our offside wheels perilously near the edge of the precipice, and with a final derisive snort from the exhaust skidded round the leader of the crocodile. As a result, we were one of the few to reach the final control without loss of marks. It looked as though we would do well in the rally, but pride came before the fall all right. I made an unholy mess of the reversing and braking tests, and it was the turn of our Bwlch-Y-Gross friends to do the deriding.

But it had been a great year; I had really passed through the transitional period of being an up and coming young driver, to being an accepted one.

III

The new year opened well. Proof of the fact that I was no longer a mere possible, but a probable, was given me on the morning of the first home race meeting of the season at Goodwood.

The London evening paper *The Star* habitually gives selections for the important race meetings, just as it does with horses, and before racing began I saw that I was tipped for the Lavant Cup and Reg Parnell for the Chichester Cup. So I was now bracketed with a man who had reached and been at the top of the tree for some time. Anyway, the tipping wasn't bad, because both of us won our respective races, though it was a close thing for me for I crossed the finishing line a mere four-fifths of a second before my old-time friend and rival, Eric Brandon.

A month later, we were off to the Continent. We had a terrific programme in front of us, starting with the Mille Miglia, which, as its name implies, is a 1,000 mile race—and what a 1,000 miles! It is certainly the most dangerous of all events. More than half the 1,000 miles of the Mille Miglia course is over twisty or mountain roads, but that did not worry us. The Jaguars had been sent over well in advance, and we had been able to put in a fair bit of practice. Of all races, however, the Mille Miglia is the most unpredictable. The roads are not completely closed, though the course extends in the form of an hour-glass from Brescia in the north to Rome in the south. But the whole of Italy knows all about it and though, for their own safety's sake, the Italians do not trespass too recklessly on the course, you never know, in the rural districts, what lies ahead of you at the next corner.

There may be children playing in the village streets, a herd of cattle, or even a drunk. Obviously, then, you must for ever be on the look-out; your nerves tensed, your feet ready to stab at the controls, sometimes the accelerator to win through a partial obstruction such as a skidding car, sometimes the brake to pull you up short of disaster.

The Italians had made a real Roman holiday of the Mille Miglia and, by reason of their successes in preceding years, had come to regard themselves as almost unbeatable. It was up to us to break down their domination of the event, but our challenge was shortlived, and it was shared by one of the greatest of all the Italians. Alberto Ascari, much fancied to win outright, spun round in the road not much more than 15 miles from the start. It was dark and the roads were wet and greasy. My car was travelling at about 115 miles an hour, when the headlights caught the frantic signals of a man ahead, waving me down. I applied the brakes—nothing happened, and that is an experience which is quite terrifying at that speed.

Down into lower gear, a turn of the steering wheel, still

no response. I was on an oil patch, with not the slightest frictional resistance between tyres and road surface. I could do nothing, and biffed the car ahead. Without having done any serious damage I reversed, continued to a garage and mended the model, but the gear jammed in reverse while backing out of the repair shop, and that was that. It took over an hour to fix. I was out of the hunt, and the well-laid plans of the Jaguar Company had gone to pot.

Leslie Johnson, driving another Jaguar ahead of me, had been victimised by the same obstruction and he had driven off the road trying to avoid adding to the blockade. It was the right thing to do, but he could not get his car back on to the road again. There were quite a lot of crashes in that race, as there almost inevitably must be in such a contest, and the Italians were able to cheer home Luigi Villoresi to retain their fine record of successes.

There was quite a deal of consolation for me, however, when Tommy Wisdom brought home an Aston Martin to win the tourist class, for it was Tommy who had helped me to my greatest triumph by giving me his car to drive in the Tourist Trophy.

In a brief spell from my Continental engagements I went back to Silverstone to compete in the Production Car race at the International meeting. My event preceded the big event of the day for Grand Prix type cars, in which there was a superb field, including Dr. Farina and Juan Fangio. The race was one of the most comfortable I had ever driven in. The Jaguar was in fine fettle; after a moderate start which left me somewhere round about fifth or sixth during the initial sprint, I began overtaking those ahead of me, and took the lead in the second lap to the finish at 85·5 miles an hour over about 100 miles.

I was followed home by three other Jaguar drivers, so that it was quite a field day for us. Then came that sensational final to the Grand Prix type race. Fangio won the first heat at over 91 miles an hour and Farina the second at over

93 m.p.h., and I had managed to qualify for the final in the completely outpaced H.W.M. Reg Parnell had nearly stolen a march on Fangio who, with a lap to go, saw the British driver close on his tail; he brought in all his horses, but was still unable to shake off Parnell, who finished only three seconds behind him. For the 35 laps final (103 miles) it looked all the world to a China orange on a first-class match between Farina and Fangio, both on Alfa Romeos, and I may say that my money was evenly divided between them.

The race started in a drizzle of rain, but before the cars could get round the first circuit it turned into one of the most heavy deluges I have ever seen in this country. It came down literally in sheets. Parking sites became lakes, enclosures were inches deep in water and the circuit was just a river. It was difficult to see anything except water. While this was happening, Reg Parnell in the 4½-litre Ferrari plunged—and that is the right word—through the waves left by the two F's, Farina and Fangio, and piloted his boat through the raging tempest ahead of them. It was not a case of car speed, but of sheer, downright courage—or perhaps "guts" is a more descriptive word. Reg was just able to tackle the conditions better than these two world champion drivers. The tropical deluge not only continued, but got worse. The stewards went into hurried consultation and after six laps—eighteen miles—called the race off. They were not to be blamed. If the race had gone on in those conditions—and they didn't abate for a long while—there might have been real disaster. Official observers from all parts of the course had reported that things were quite impossible, the timekeepers could not see to "clock" the competitors and those drivers in front, especially Reg Parnell, were driving almost blind. It seemed dreadful bad luck for Parnell that the race should have been abandoned, but very soon the stewards announced that the prizes would be awarded to those holding the premier positions at the call-off, so that Reg was returned as the official winner of what must have been the shortest international race in the history of the game.

It was the first time in my experience that a race once having started had been abandoned, but it was completely justifiable and the very big crowd at Silverstone approved of the decision. There were about 100,000 spectators, but if the race had gone on, not one per cent of that mighty concourse would have seen anything except spray.

IV

The next big race was the Italian Grand Prix de Auto-drome at Monza, for Formula 2 cars. The cars were 2 litres without superchargers. Italy was there in all its strength with Fangio, Villoresi and Ascari aboard a very fast team of Ferraris. The regulations were rather unusual in that the race was run in two heats of nearly 100 miles each, and the result decided on the aggregate time for both heats. I was driving an H.W.M. which, though nothing like as fast as the Italian cars, was beginning to make its presence felt in international racing.

Away went the three Ferraris with Ascari in the lead and Fangio doing everything he could to take it away from him, but for once Fangio overdid it. He discovered the fact that too many revs. have to be paid for, and he was soon out of the hunt with a protesting engine. Villoresi was now second, and I tucked in behind him to enjoy a tow in his slip-stream for nearly the whole of the race. As I have said before, you do not do this except when you are slip-streaming a master, and Villoresi is. Round and round we went, with the Italian taking his corners faster and faster in an effort to drop me; but up went my revs., up to the official maximum and up went my speed, until towards the end Villoresi managed to get by a slower car and leave me in the lurch; so I tucked in behind Trintignant on a Gordini and he carried me home in fourth place, which wasn't bad for a car which was normally outpaced by many of the cars behind it.

The second heat was a repetition of the first, only more so —much more so. It was almost like a paced race, with all the fast men except the leader slip-streaming somebody or other. Again I re-requisitioned the services of Villoresi, and again he proved to be a first-class pacemaker. My maximum speed was reputed to be 130 miles an hour, and joyously I saw my rev. counter go on to 5,900 instead of its theoretical 5,400, which meant I was getting a 10-miles-an-hour "lift" from Villoresi at 140 miles an hour.

He didn't try any tricks except that ever-increasing speed on the corners, but I did my best to match him drift for drift and it must have been quite exciting to the spectators to see the two of us tearing round as though there were a tow-rope between us. Of course, I had to be on the alert the whole time, ready to cope with any emergency that might happen. Villoresi drove faultlessly and eventually won, but though Ascari was able to pass me I finished in third place and was placed in the same position on aggregate, which was a feather in the bonnet of the British H.W.M. in such company.

3

DOG FIGHT IN THE RAIN

I

BACK again to England for a Goodwood meeting and a 500 c.c. race in which I drove a Kieft in its first outing. I nearly experienced ignominy, for somebody had omitted to change the soft practice plugs to the hard racing ones and there I was, sweating and fuming, completely outpaced. I just managed to qualify for the final by finishing eighth in the heat, the last of the qualifying places. What a difference when I got the hard plugs in! It was as though previously somebody had "doped" my car, and now I was able to win easily, putting up the fastest lap at 84·5 m.p.h. I must say these little 500's are really fast—and participating in £200 prize and bonus money is quite a little sweetener.

Air travel has enabled those of us who race cars to fulfil much bigger programmes than we otherwise would, but, fast as they are, they give nothing like the impression of speed that one gets on terra firma. The spectacle and the feeling of speed are relative. A car travelling to 40 m.p.h. in a narrow lane seems to be travelling as fast as one doing 60 on an arterial road, both to the spectator and to the driver.

I had a couple of fruitless races at Genoa a little later, breaking the suspension in the 500 c.c. race when leading and then smashing the differential in the Formula 2 race. If I were axiomatic I would say that these things are sent to try us, but they are not. They are all part of the game, and I was now an old enough hand to realise that you can't always have the luck.

(*Above*): Stirling Moss receives his first Gold Star award from Earl Howe, President of the British Racing Drivers' Club. Moss has won the Gold Star, which represents the British Championship award, six times for the years 1950/51/52/54/55/56.

(*Below*): Silverstone 1951: with an XK 120 Jaguar in the Sports Car Race, which Stirling won. He also won "The Race of the Champions" at the same meeting in another Jaguar XK 120.
(*Photo: T. C. March*)

(*Above*): Stirling Moss driving Kieft No. 7 at the start of the 500 c.c. race at Silverstone, 1951. This car, designed by Ray Martin, the late John Cooper and D. H. Delamont, employed many unconventional features in Formula 3 design and achieved a long string of victories in Stirling's hands.
(*Photo: T. C. March*)

(*Below*): Unloading the BRM at Monza, Northern Italy, where Stirling spent many weeks testing for the BRM organisation in an effort to diagnose the car's many faults. (*Photo: Acme*)

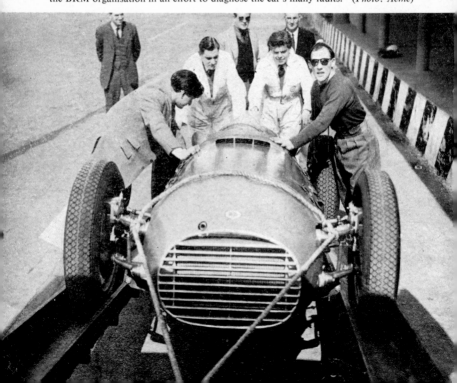

In spite of my failures, the critics continued to call me the boy driver, the budding Nuvolari. I must say that I regarded myself as quite mature, but then my father, who accompanied me on most of my trips, was like a two-year-old himself, running the pits, jubilant when I was winning, actively helping me when I was in trouble. How could the son of anybody so young be other than a boy?

Soon after the Genoa débâcle I was back again on the Continent for the Swiss Grand Prix on the Bremgarten Circuit at Berne. Of all the European courses I think this is about the most dangerous, difficult and interesting. Though there are few real straights, it is fast, which means that most of the corners and curves can be taken at speed. In the excitement of the race, it is only too easy to go a little too fast. I didn't fall into that trap, but I had a most hair-raising—and that is the right term— experience.

Early in the race a stone shattered my windscreen, which would have been bad enough in any circumstances, but there was a howling gale and torrential rain. On the faster stretches I had to hold my helmet on with one hand (that's why "hair-raising" is so apt), while the rain almost cut into my face. This went on for about an hour and a half, but somehow I managed to keep reasonably among the leaders, though my H.W.M. was very much slower than the Ferraris or Alfa Romeos. At any rate, I led all the British cars, but then, not more than about 300 yards from the finish, I ran out of petrol, and while I coasted in, Louis Chiron on a Maserati pipped me for sixth place.

But what a race it was. There was a real dog fight in the vanguard between Fangio, Farina, Taruffi and Ascari. The brilliant Fangio held the lead almost throughout after a masterly demonstration of race driving in bad weather, and it looked for all the world as though the man on whom I had modelled myself, Farina, would follow him home in second place, but in the penultimate lap, Taruffi went absolutely

B 33

crazy in his Ferrari, snaked by Farina and so split the two Alfa Romeo drivers.

Just by way of a little comic relief from this chancy business, what about this for a contrasting interlude? I had engaged to drive in a night trial through the Chilterns, and my car was a little Morris Minor. It turned out to be a nice little nocturne in Moss Minor, for I lost fifty marks because I made a mistake in map reading. Thank goodness one doesn't have to have maps on race tracks.

II

Back to Europe for racing at Aix les Bains. In the first heat, the Italian driver Cortese did a full-circle pirouette in the road just as I was about to overtake him. Though I hit his spinning car, mine seemed to be all right; I went on to finish first, but it wasn't so funny in the final, as the steering seemed a bit peculiar. It transpired that the front wheels were out of track. However, I managed to bring the H.W.M. into second place.

On to Rome and then to the Isle of Man for the British Empire Trophy. About this time I rather changed my mind and from now on I considered Fangio the first driver in the world.

The British Empire event was decided on handicap, and I was one of the back markers in a relatively little known car to me, a Frazer Nash. Again the course was of the "round-the-houses" type in Douglas, having to be covered thirty-five times for a distance of 136 miles. My job was to overtake the smaller cars with, as it always seemed to the scratch men, their colossal lead. I was going quite well and streaked through the field, but with no hope of catching Pat Griffiths. Both of us had escaped a pile-up of about half a dozen cars early in the race, and towards the closing stages it looked as though I would be an easy second, but with no chance of overtaking the leader. Then along came Lady

Luck, frowned at Pat and smiled at me. Griffiths had me absolutely whacked with two laps to go, but then his engine petered out and I was able to roll home a comfortable winner.

Then came one of the real classics of the year, the Le Mans 24-Hour race, an event which calls for terrific endurance, There is nothing quite like Le Mans, with its festival atmosphere and the high enthusiasm of the spectators who throng the circuit day and night. The famous Le Mans start has been imitated copiously. It consists of lining up on one side of the road and, on the starting signal, to dash across to your car, start up the engine and do your utmost to get among the leaders so as to enjoy the advantage of a clear course. "Lofty" England, chief of the Jaguar pits control, gave Jack Fairman, my co-driver, and myself our marching orders. We were to be the pacemakers, the men whose job it was to try to crack up the opposition; quite a compliment, but rather dimming race-winning prospects.

Motor-racing tactics, especially in such long-distance events as the Le Mans 24-Hours, are not unlike those which occur on the athletic track between milers. It is run as a team with a pacemaker to try to upset the opposition, and his colleague or colleagues coming along to take up the final sprint. Le Mans is for sports cars, but these are not much slower than the Grand Prix type racers, and such is the importance of success to the firms supporting it that the services of the very best drivers are sought. As I said, Jack and I had to be pacemakers to a talented and experienced crowd of "dicers". We had done quite well in practice and had learned most of the tricks of the circuit. It is just under $8\frac{1}{2}$ miles in length, with just about all the varieties of curves there are, only, unlike film-star figures, the curves aren't always in the right places. On leaving the pits and passing beneath Dunlop Bridge, there is a fast curve which leads to the Esses which, as the name implies, is a twisty section. A fast sharp right-hander at Tertre Rouge leads into the

Mulsanne Straight, where you can really put your foot down and get the maximum revs.

Near the end of the straight there is a very difficult right curve. Then Mulsanne corner slows you up, and is followed by another fast section to a right and left corner taken at about 70 m.p.h. Then comes Arnage, the slowest turn of the lot, and where quite a lot of crashes have occurred. After this, one accelerates to top gear and then negotiates a fast left and right over a brow, which is very difficult at night as one's lights shine up in the air. Down a slight hill to Whitehouse, a fast and difficult right and left swerve; now a fast straight to the pits and start-finish line.

You start winning the Le Mans race long before the event begins because you have to discuss beforehand strategy, tactics, speed, maintenance, signalling, etc.; even before that, the cars have to be prepared in the factory, with a particular eye to gear ratios to suit the circuit, and to petrol consumption, which means planning the pit stops for replenishments. When you arrive for practice, you can be well assured that the car is in top-notch condition, but as a result of practice laps, modifications may be necessary. Anyway, there we were at Le Mans with a team of Jaguars intent on breaking the long sequence of foreign victories. We were feared, I think, more than any other British cars since the famous Bentley boys had won in 1935—sixteen years before.

Our practice times seemed to justify French fears, though Louis Rosier on a big 4½-litre Talbot was confidently expected to bring home the tricolour ahead of the Union Jack. During the first practice period I put in a lap at 5 minutes dead, which was considered good enough by the team manager, but I think he thought even more of a 5 minutes 11 seconds lap accomplished in rain and mist. I had one practice experience which brought home to me the absolute need of concentrating to the utmost. I had crossed the brow of a hill at a good two miles a minute to find the road ahead partially blocked by a German Porsche car upside down and

Mort Goodall looking for an opening in an Aston Martin. As I arrived he found one, and assisted by my Jaguar bumping him, he shot through. It was quite a close thing.

On the eve of the race, Rosier was interviewed on his chances by French journalists, and said: "I fear the British Jaguars more than anything else." Then came the final conference. "Lofty" England was the skipper, and it was then he told us that we were to be wreckers-in-chief and try to break up the opposition. He also gave us a lecture about signals so that we should thoroughly understand them.

If we were to be pacemakers, then obviously we should have to get away to a good start, or I might get crowded in. The weather was rotten, and it got worse. I was badly placed for the getaway, for at the line-up my car was twenty-second in the row, standing diagonally in echelon with the rest of the field. We were all on the other side of the road ready for the starter's signal, and when it came I sprinted to my car; not a long sprint, but enough to give me a slight advantage, as I am quite quick on my feet. I was in the driver's seat and away, passing fourteen cars before anybody else had moved.

The big American Cunninghams and Talbots were in front of me, and I chased them round, gaining all the time until on the Mulsanne Straight I took the lead. There I was correctly positioned to try to make it hot for anybody who passed. At the end of the straight, Gonzales, the dashing South American driver on one of the big Talbots, beat me on braking at the bend. I kept close to him and passed him before the straight. My car was the faster and I could have increased my lead; but orders is orders, as they ay in the classics, so I tantalisingly kept the margin down and, at Tertre Rouge, let him use his brakes hard again to snatch the lead. This technique went on for five laps, a proper piece of cat-and-mouse stuff. Then Gonzales slowed with his brakes finished. I think I must have grinned to myself at the success of the ruse, and for a time I had quite a little motoring in the lead, though the field had spread out and there was a deal of braking and acceleration as I passed slower competitors.

The Jaguar held that road like a leech. It was grand. There was nobody to break up as instructed, and I was in my element. Because of the stability of the car I was able to take the two right-hand bends between Mulsanne and Arnage full bore, and I leaped over the brow of the hill just before White House at 130 miles an hour. For eight hours everything went as merrily as the proverbial wedding bells. Then my heart sank because the oil-pressure indicator was doing the same thing. An oil-pipe had broken, and gradually the car subsided to a full stop, leaving me three miles from the pits on a narrow portion of the circuit. Nothing for it but to walk home in the pouring rain, and that wasn't at all funny, because every time the lights of a car signalled the approach of a competitor I had to jump off the road into the ditch, and that damnable ditch was full of water. You don't stop to choose when the selection is between getting a soaking and getting knocked down by a racing car.

I reached the pits at two o'clock in the morning, which is as good a time as any to feel unhappy, but they gave me a great welcome. I had done my share of the job and had beaten the record for the course. Everybody was jubilant, for sticking out in front now were Peter Walker and Peter Whitehead in another Jaguar, and there they stayed until the finish, to win with a distance of 2,244 miles at an average speed of 93·49 miles an hour. There were 150,000 other people to cheer them across the line as the National Anthem was played. After sixteen years the great Le Mans race had come back to England, and real racing glory had come to Mr. (now Sir) William Lyons, chief of the Jaguar firm.

I drew a couple of blanks after Le Mans, for after two laps in the Avus race, Berlin, I broke a connecting-rod and at the Rouen Grand Prix a few days later, gear-box trouble eliminated me after 27 laps. Then we had some fun on the Kieft.

It started at Silverstone in the 500 c.c. curtain-raiser, where I knocked the record down to under two minutes for a complete circuit at an average of 87 miles an hour and won fairly easily. Next week was Zandvoort where the Kieft won again.

A few weeks later it was Germany, and I took the all-con-quering Kieft there, but it was no walk-over this time. On the night before the race I was violently ill, probably as a result of some food or other that had disagreed with me, and I had to be given drugs. I felt fairly fit the next day, and started well enough by collecting a nice little 20 seconds' lead on the first lap, which I doubled at the end of the second circuit; then the steering arm broke and I had to bring the car to a standstill, but not before I had beaten the lap record, for which they gave me a handsome cigar-case—wish I smoked cigars.

Events happened so quickly that I seemed to be dashing about almost as fast between races as during them. Within a few days of being at Nurburgring I found myself at Freiburg for an international hill climb; this was my first experience of this kind of sport on the Continent, though, as you will have read, I had more or less started my career on English hills. Freiburg is really fantastic with over 100 bends in an eight-mile climb. The arrangements were that cars should be sent up at one-minute intervals, but with such a long climb ahead of me, the officials gave me a three minutes' margin. It was just as well, because that hill really suited my Kieft and I stormed up it in 8 minutes 32 seconds to wipe nearly a minute off the record.

I had an odd experience shortly afterwards. To my de-light I was invited by the Ferrari firm to drive one of their cars in the Bari Grand Prix. I flew to Italy all keyed up with excitement at driving a car from such a stable in a Grand Prix event. But apparently there was some misunderstanding. It seemed that there would have been something of an outcry if I had been allowed to drive in place of the popular Taruffi, a home-bred star. So I was just a spectator, but the journey was not wasted, as I saw Juan Fangio win a beautiful race.

About this time the B.R.M. was engaging everybody's attention, and I must say I was very keen on this honest-to-goodness attempt to build a Grand Prix car, British through and through, which would give battle to the all-conquering Italians.

At the back of my mind was the cherished hope for recognition; the daydream that my services would be sought by one of the crack stables. I think my mind's eye was focused on the B.R.M. Never had a car been so lauded and so condemned. It was reported that something like £250,000 had been spent on the project in an attempt to show our flag in the big Continental races. Over two years had been spent in perfecting it, but all it had earned so far was ignominy. Yet I was fascinated by it. Success had eluded it, but that fantastic scream of its engine drummed in my ears. My immediate ambition was to drive that ill-fated car and get the chequered flag against the might of foreign cars and personnel in a great Continental classic.

I was not impatient. I knew many of the problems inseparable from the perfection of a Grand Prix car; I knew about the "bugs" that had to be got rid of, and I knew the difficulty of making decisions, such as whether to race the car without being certain of its preparedness or whether to withhold participation until finality had been reached. I had not long to wait. I was invited to go and see Mr. Raymond Mays, principal of the B.R.M. enterprise, at Bourne, and discuss with him plans for me to join the official team. He had expressed the opinion, in print, that he wanted me to drive the B.R.M. and it was arranged that I should take over the car on the Folkingham Airfield in Lincolnshire and try it out.

Glory be, the chance I had been waiting for! And, as so often seems to happen, along came an alternative and attractive proposition. I was asked by the all-conquering Ferrari management if I would like to join their Grand Prix team. So it all happened at once; from being a good prospect I had become an accepted exponent of motor racing in its highest element. Naturally I would prefer to drive a British car, and the B.R.M. looked a good bet. Could I remove the hoodoo? The car had done fairly well at Silverstone; admittedly its drivers, Reg Parnell and Peter Walker, had suffered untold agony owing to leg burns from the cockpit, but that was just another bug which, having been discovered, would be eliminated. Well, there I was on the way to the Lincolnshire runways to "show off my paces" to a very critical group. My instructions were to take it easy until I had really got the feel of the car. The importance of the occasion worried me a bit, but I had to take her out and I was soon touching the high spots, getting from her a higher speed than I had ever reached before, something around the 180's.

The critics announced that they were impressed; I was passed as a sufficiently capable driver to handle the car and plans were made for me to take it to Monza and experiment with it on what was probably the finest testing ground available. There was also the Ferrari proposition to be considered. It seemed certain that in the following year I would take my place among the fully-fledged G.P. drivers. The Ferrari offer was acclaimed by the Press as a sort of insignia of honour in that I was the first British driver who had been invited to join a foreign racing team since the war.

The B.R.M. was prepared for action and sent down to Monza, and there I went, not as a potential driver to have his qualifications tested, but as a test driver to see and report on what the car would do.

On my first run I was able to lap at over 115 m.p.h., but

the car behaved badly. We had many problems to iron out. Could the car be a real threat to the Continental teams? Exhaustive tests were carried out, modifications were decided upon and finality appeared on the near horizon. There was no doubt at all about the power development of the car, but there were other snags which needed a probe. It was decided to enter for the Italian Grand Prix at Monza, especially as the resident track manager had commented favourably on the car. He declared that it was comparable with the fastest of the Alfa Romeos, but he also said that England would have to find more drivers. "Reg Parnell and Stirling Moss, splendid as they are," he said, "do not constitute a team. Before you can hope to win Grand Prix races you must find drivers of the same calibre as Fangio."

But the long sequence of misfortunes was not yet at an end. The B.R.M.s were withdrawn just before the Italian classic owing to transmission trouble which developed during pre-race tests. Incidentally, there was something of a sensation. Ken Richardson, chief tester to B.R.M., was given the second car to drive in the race, but at the last moment official word came from the Royal Automobile Club that he was not to start. The reason given was that the parent club did not think that he had had sufficient experience to take part in such an event.

For a while we carried on with the H.W.M., which, if it did not have the maximum gait of the Continental G.P. cars, was more than holding its own. I drove one in the Wakefield Trophy race organised by the Irish Motor Racing Club on the Curragh Circuit. Driving a similar car was Duncan Hamilton, a very experienced and very daring driver. The event was a double-barrelled affair with major prizes for scratch and handicap winners. The first lap was a dog fight with me in the lead and Robert Baird, an Irish newspaper proprietor, close up. Newspaper men are difficult to shake off, and so I discovered with Bobby Baird. I was getting along the fast straight at just over two miles a minute, but there was the Irishman still on my heels—or wheels. Then he disappeared from the fray and another Irishman, J. Kelly, took up the chase, but I was out in front and luckily they didn't head me off. Four times I equalled the record for the course, and in the final lap I broke it by two seconds at 83·51 miles an hour. As a result, I brought off the double, winning the scratch event and the handicap.

4

GREMLINS ON MY BACK

I

MOTOR racing had now attained a greater popularity than ever it had enjoyed before, and new circuits were springing up like mushrooms all over the country. Fine; what more could a professional racer want? My foreign engagements prevented me from racing at a new circuit at Boreham in Essex, but I loaned my Kieft to Eric Brandon and earmarked Boreham for a future visit.

By this time the Tourist Trophy race had come round again, and, naturally, I was very anxious to win an event which had brought my biggest triumph the year before. If I could win again, I would join the great Tazio Nuvolari and the impish Freddie Dixon as the only "dicers" who have won the classic twice. I was part of the official Jaguar team and I could not have wished for a better mount. It was the XK120 type on which, earlier in the year, Peter Whitehead and Peter Walker had won at Le Mans. Cars of all sizes and descriptions were in the event, all of them production models, plus some rather important modifications. The race was a handicap, with time and distance allowances being given in accordance with engine capacity.

Bad weather conditions during practice were replaced by a fine race day and, having really trained for the event, I felt as fit as a fiddle. My car was No. 7, and I don't mind admitting that that helped, because not only is it my favourite number, but like most drivers, whether they admit it or not, I am a bit superstitious. Not for the first time I had asked to be allotted that number. Later on, when I was driving Grand Prix cars, superstition led me to be rather sorry that the British racing colour should be green.

I can tell you of all sorts of manifestations of superstition on the part of race drivers. The late Sir Malcolm Campbell would not drive a car, racing or touring, unless it carried the badge of St. Christopher, and he had all his cars painted blue, a result of his seeing Maeterlinck's play the *Blue Bird*, which was the title he bestowed on all his record breakers. Prince Birabongse, better known as Bira, favours a Mickey Mouse for an emblem, and the late Sir Tim Birkin always wore a white-spotted blue scarf. There are men with a sort of obverse superstition who ask for No. 13, which normally is not allotted on a race entry list, and send in their entry on a Friday.

Anyway, there was I on the line in a big field, ready for the 45 laps and 319 miles. Though I was still only twenty-one, I was no longer a mere "up and coming" young driver; I was in fact one of the favourites for the event, doubtless because of my success in 1950.

Everything went according to plan. My job was to get credit points over the time allowance on which the handicap was framed. Immediately I began to get those valuable credit points, and the race had not been going for long when the satisfying signal came from the pits: "You are leading-plus"—the plus meaning that I was ahead of schedule. I suppose racing motorists, like footballers or cricketers or any other sports participants feel, at times, that they are at the top of their form. Well, I did on that day. It was as though I could not make a mistake. The corners seemed to ease out; the car seemed brilliantly responsive to every control. I took the lead in the first lap and, with the car weaving in and out on the road to pass slower-moving competitors, I stayed in front to the end, winning at 83·55 miles an hour, which was very much faster than my 1950 time. So it should have been, because the ideal conditions this time contrasted acutely with the foul weather in which I had won my first T.T.

The Press was very extravagant in their praise over that race. One paper declared that my "two-thirds of a hat trick" was a greater achievement than those of Nuvolari or Dixon because, whereas they were both seasoned campaigners, "Moss hadn't sat in a racing car more than a few years and he had won the first two T.T.s in which he had competed". I think perhaps the biggest bouquet came from a French paper whose report of the race was headed "British Nuvolari Wins Again".

From Ireland to Goodwood for the Autumn International meeting, Farina being among the competitors. I collected three firsts, two with Jaguars and the other on an H.W.M. but failed to bring home a fourth race, a handicap, being pipped on the post by Farina.

Racing is not always deadly serious rivalry. At Brands Hatch, which is a circuit shaped something like a pair of spectacles, with a natural amphitheatre for spectators on the surrounding hills, I had qualified for the 25 laps final. This was quite an easy race, because my Kieft was much faster than anything else on the track. So it proved; I had lapped most of the competitors when, just for the fun of the thing, I waved to Derek Annable, a friend of mine, to get into my slip-stream so that I could give him a tow. Derek had made a bad start and was somewhere in the rearguard, so he accepted my invitation and I carried him through most of the field, before waving good-bye to go on and win at the new record average of 66·91 miles an hour.

That was about the end of the racing season that year. Just to cap a satisfying year's racing, the Gold Star of the British Racing Drivers' Club came my way. I think I may regard 1951 as my year of transition; the year in which I passed from the queue at the barrier to the arrival platform. Yet the fact remained that I had not been at the wheel of a real G.P. car in a real Grand Prix race.

II

By now I was probably the only full-time professional driver in the country; nearly all the others having some other commercial interest, some garage proprietors, others farmers. But my education was not yet complete. There were several events in which I had not yet competed, and one of them was the famous Monte Carlo rally, a classic event in which British drivers and cars had not done very well in the past. Indeed, the only two Britishers to have won it had achieved their victories in the long distant past.

So far as racing in the New Year was concerned, there came some attractive offers from Continental firms and a definite invitation to join the official Ferrari team, but for the time being I preferred to take my chance with the B.R.M. Monza, which I revisited for further research work, had shown me that for sheer power the B.R.M. was a potential world beater. The steering wasn't so good, with quite a bit of back lash, but that was something I hoped could easily be put right. If the B.R.M. were stationary and a car passed it at 120 m.p.h., the British car could overtake it within a mile. That was the sort of acceleration it had. As it happened, everybody was rather over-anxious to have a British world winner, and gave it more credit than it deserved.

Before the year was out, I had been asked if I would like to lead a team as part of the entry of the Sunbeam Talbot concern for the Monte Carlo Rally. I accepted readily and very soon was learning something about thoroughness in preparation. The manager, organiser and brains of the party was Norman Garrad, a very experienced rallier. First, all the Sunbeam drivers were ordered to a conference; it was like going to school again. There we were, about thirty of us, in a lecture-room whose walls were surrounded by maps and itineraries. We were told how to cope with all sorts of weather conditions; how the art of conforming to schedule in a rally was a very different thing from racing. We were told how necessary it was to train for the event. Every conceivable contingency was considered, diagnosed and proper remedies to apply were thrashed out. We were told that our cars would be put into the finest possible condition and that it was up to us that we did the same. I would like to say here that I think Norman Garrad is possibly the greatest organiser for Rally participation that there is. Like Neubauer, he is liked and respected by his drivers and mechanics.

Co-drivers with me in the Monte were John Cooper of the *Autocar* and Desmond Scannell, Secretary of the British Racing Drivers' Club. Orders from Skipper Garrad were that we should start from Monte Carlo, which, of the several routes available, seemed to contain the more difficult sections in the early stages. The general idea was that after having accomplished part of the rally from their chosen starting points, the competitors should link up into a single route for the closing stages.

My co-drivers paid me the compliment of asking me to drive in the difficult sectors, and the weather conditions saw to it that normal hazards were greatly accentuated by the snow, frozen ruts and solid ice over which we had to drive, sometimes flat out, in order to keep up with schedule. It was, as I have said, my first Monte Carlo rally, so I had no sort of standard by which to judge the relative conditions, but it turned out to be more arduous and dangerous than any that had preceded it. There were crashes everywhere and I must say I was not surprised when I heard about them. Even before the start, in the principality of Monaco itself, snow was falling, a most unheard of thing; I could not help laughing at the indignation of the natives at such a phenomenal visitation. They set to work to clear it away as though some scourge had lighted on the country.

Just to add to the difficulties under wheel, there were fog

patches in the mountains, and if you want to know what
"hazardous" means, try fast driving on ice with visibility
reduced to a few yards and the prospect of a disabled car
blocking the road ahead of you. If my co-drivers got a
bit "windy" during part of that drive, I'm not surprised.
It is very much less of a strain on the driver's nerves than
on those of the passengers when you are doing a spot of
over-the-safety-margin motoring.

By the time we joined up with the other ralliers for the
Liége–Amsterdam, Brussels–Paris circuit and the event had
become a whole instead of a series of independent cavalcades,
we were in the best of humours, We had not lost a single
mark. The rest of the rally was going to be a bit easier, so
we thought, but it got worse; it became almost unendurable.
We had a few first-class little through-town races at Amsterdam, the Hague and Paris, where we were escorted by motor-
cycle mounted police who entered into the spirit of the thing
with knobs on. They took no notice at all of traffic signals
or anything else, but blinded along as though they were
competing in some sort of "round-the-houses" race. Many
of the competing cars reached Paris with spectacular evidence
of the ordeal through which they had passed. There were
smashed wings, broken headlights and, in some cases, almost
completely wrecked bodies. The going was not so bad on
the southward run to Bourges, but after that the position
grew even worse! Snow began to fall heavily on the ice-
bound roads, and there is no more treacherous top dressing
to a road than that.

Soon it was a complete shambles. Dozens of cars lay
in all sorts of positions in the roadside ditches; others were
completely stranded, with their drivers quite unable to get
the wheels to grip. Louis Chiron, the veteran French racing
ace, was ditched, and as a rescue squad tried to drag his
car back to the road at the end of a rope, another competitor
came round the bend, the rescuers jumped for their lives
and Chiron's car slipped back into the ditch again.

Some frightening incidents occurred in front of us; cars crashed; others, which you could just see out of the corner of your eye, hung perilously over precipices, and still others were locked in an unhappy embrace by the roadside; a real Dante's inferno on ice.

Just a little comic relief: an Italian, whose car was well and truly ditched, implored help from a British car. He got it, and with wheels spinning round the car crept forward at walking pace. Then the wheels gripped and as the car got away the Italian was left gesticulating wildly and frantically. The British competitor did not discover until he reached the next control that the Italian had fixed his one and only tow-rope to the back and there it was, tailing along behind in the snow.

Not so amusing was Ken Wharton's experience. Here was a famous driver who was involved in one of the many crashes as a direct result of uncontrollable meteorological conditions. Ken's car skidded violently, went over the edge and landed on another car which had gone over the edge earlier. Beneath that French car was another one, so there were three wrecked cars lying on a steep slope, one on top of the other and a drop of over 100 feet just below them.

Finally, we came to Journey's End at Monte Carlo. Nearly a hundred had started from Monte Carlo with us, but no others got through. Only about 100 of the 300-odd competitors completed the journey, and a mere sixteen cars checked in at the finish without loss of marks. Ours was one of them.

All depended on the Regularity Test, with only myself and Sydney Allard, driving a car of his own manufacture, as the British "full markers". This decider was over a 45-mile circuit on the notorious Col de Brause, and what a snorter it was. The zigzag, mountainous course was just as treacherous as it could have been, and the contest became more of a skidding match than anything else. Indeed, the conditions were so bad that the officials decided to reduce the average speed to 28 miles an hour and though it may not sound like it, that meant all-out nearly all the time. I slid off the road into a mound of snow, and John and Des spent an unhappy and hectic 40-odd seconds pushing the car back on to the road again. Sydney had a narrower escape from failure, for he hit a brick wall and severely bent the front of the model, but found he was able to drive on.

Finally we both finished, and Sydney Allard won. Both of us had exceeded our schedule; Sydney by 2 seconds and me by 4 seconds, so one of the most difficult rallies ever held, over a distance of about 2,000 miles, was won by that 2 seconds miscalculation of speed. Sounds a bit like the tail wagging the dog, but Sydney Allard deserved to win, and we hadn't done so badly by backing up so closely the first British winner for many years.

In rallies the same as racing, a team is necessary, and without men like John and Des, who incidentally did all the brain work, one might just as well not start.

III

There I was, doing quite well with a full season ahead of me, but just as I was hoping for more good runs, the clouds began to gather. I experienced a run of bad luck of the sort that comes to everybody now and then. Nothing seemed to go right. I had reckoned to do quite a lot with the B.R.M. in the Grand Prix series, but then first one country, then another decided that its G.P. events would be for Formula 2 cars, for which the B.R.M. was not eligible. Undoubtedly there would be a few national or international events to suit it, and there would also be Formula Libre, that is to say, free for all size. After a lot of consideration I decided that I would accept the offer of leading the B.R.M. team, instead of accepting the tentative offers made by a couple of Continental firms.

I went along to Bourne, the lair of the B.R.M., to get measured, for you need fitting for a car as for a suit. The steering pillar was shortened to allow for my "long arm" position at the driving wheel and the cockpit was "styled" to suit my requirements. You cannot race a car properly unless you are comfortable. Already I had experienced the discomfort of sitting in a driver's seat which was intended for a bigger posterior than mine.

It wasn't until I had won a few "bread-and-butter" events at the various tracks, Goodwood and Castle Combe among them, with one or two lap records to my credit, that the hoodoo first made its appearance. Just about everything that could happen on a race track began to happen to me. These things seem to run in series, but nothing that has happened in the past can alter the law of chance in the future. At roulette, for example, black may win in a long sequence; but however long that sequence, it remains an even-money chance as to whether red or black will register on the next throw.

The first of the big events was the Mille Miglia. I had actually entered for the Royal Automobile Club's big rally, but had to withdraw because of my Continental commitments. These included more experimental work with the B.R.M. at Monza. About this time I suffered what the critics regarded as a reduction in rank, but which, in fact, was nothing of the sort. The B.R.M. concern had signed on Juan Fangio as No. 1 driver, and I had been "relegated" to second driver. I should think so too. I was still a raw recruit in real Grand Prix racing, while Fangio was the world's champion. I was honoured to play second fiddle to such a leader. It was an association which was to ripen with the years, and which was to help me enormously, for Fangio taught me a great deal about racing.

So then to the Mille Miglia. My car was a C type Jaguar, and there wasn't any doubt about it being one of the fastest cars in the race. The Germans, re-entering the arena of classic racing after a long lapse, had a most impressive team in the field, but I was able to get among them in the van-guard and was lying well up. When I was passed by Kling on a fast stretch at over 150 miles an hour I felt it would be difficult to beat off the Germans.

Then it happened. With about 150 miles to go, the steering came adrift, and I was out of it. Italy regained supremacy in their beloved "Miglia" with a Ferrari beating off the German, Kling, for first place. It was a disastrous race with something like 100 accidents reported, two of them being fatal. We had our share of honours, however, for Tommy Wisdom brought home his Aston Martin to win the "Tourist" class once again.

The month of May saw me back again at Silverstone, a circuit which I had come to know so well. Indeed, what golfers call local knowledge is just as important in motor racing. The meeting was the International Trophy affair, organised by the *Daily Express*, a paper which has given enthusiastic support to motor racing, and has done much to create popular interest.

The crowd was estimated at 125,000, so that it was, apart from the Derby, one of the biggest attended sports meetings ever held. It was remarkable for two events. In the first place, Lance Macklin, whom we all knew as a brilliant driver but whose name was not very well known to the public, won the major event on an H.W.M. against strong opposition, and so brought off one of the very few British successes that had been recorded in international racing. The other notable fact about the meeting was that it brought into the limelight a man whose name was to become famous throughout the motor-racing world. Earlier in the year, tall, fair Mike Hawthorn had surprised everybody at Goodwood by winning the Lavant Cup and the Chichester Cup races. His car was a Cooper which had been super-tuned by his father, a clever engineer, but the critics quite rightly attributed Hawthorn's successes to his own driving prowess.

Silverstone was a different kettle of fish from Goodwood, and I should think most of the fans were at first curious rather than convinced about Hawthorn's driving. . But not for long. He won the first of the international heats on his Cooper, and proved that his was no flash in the pan at Goodwood. He had what it takes to make a champion driver, and subsequent events proved this to be so.

I started racing on that day with the jinx still perched on my shoulder. In the 500 c.c. "curtain-raiser" I pulled away from the field, put in a record lap and then, with three laps to go, just when things were hopeful, the nipple of the brake cable pulled off and I had to drive with the brakes partially on, which is no way to win a race. I managed to finish third, but there was consolation to follow. There were two production car races, one for touring cars and the other for sports cars, and I drove a Jaguar in each of these. It is always a good thing to sprint for the lead, and I did this. I collared the lead in the first lap, but with Ken Wharton chasing me all the way round, couldn't afford to let up. He spurred me on to another lap record, and I won at 75 m.p.h.

Switching over from the Mark VII to the C Type, I soon found myself waiting for the signal to dash across the road for a Le Mans start in the sports car event. Again I was first away, and though Peter Walker pipped me on Copse Corner I passed him soon after, kept the lead throughout and won fairly easily at 87 m.p.h. I thought I had knocked that nasty little jinx for six, with two firsts and a third, but I was wrong.

As soon as the sports car race was over, I had to dash for a racing engagement in Belgium, and get to Brussels for the Belgian Grand Prix meeting by air a couple of hours or so after leaving Silverstone.

Jinx, hoodoo, or gremlin came with me. I got off to a slow start due to having the wrong fuel, but was beating along in hot pursuit of the leaders until, as I rounded a bend, there was a pile-up of cars immediately in my path—ten or eleven all tangled up together, with not the slightest chance of my getting by them. At the side of the track was an inviting-looking row of straw bales, and since these are much softer than a mass of metal, I slammed on the brakes, skidded the car round and made for the bales. It was a bull's eye, but I was travelling at a rate of knots and the Kieft I was driving turned a complete somersault and was badly wrecked, though I was flung clear to escape unhurt. Bad news travels fast, so I took the earliest opportunity of phoning Dad at Tring to assure him that I was unscratched. I did not want him shocked by the stories about a British driver's narrow escape.

IV

Luxembourg was the next stop in a high-speed Continental tour, with another Kieft. In first-class condition on a fast track I chalked up a "first" in a preliminary heat at 116·810 k.p.h., which left me optimistic about the final. But the hoodoo was still around. He crawled into the engine, stole some of the horses and put an end to my aspirations. I finished sixth, but the race was a walk-over for British 500's, with Les Leston leading a procession of our cars ahead of all other comers.

Next stop was Berne, for the Swiss Grand Prix, with a team of H.W.M. cars there to challenge foreign supremacy. It was a fiasco ; the hoodoo again. Two of our cars, developing some sort of constructional trouble, shed their rear wheels and crashed. It was no good asking for trouble, and our pit manager, fearful that the same thing might happen again, flagged me in about half-way through the race and instructed me to drive into the dead car park.

Talk about premonition ; it was amazing, but precisely the same thing did occur in my next race and at a time when I was leading the field. It was on the Nurburgring in the sports car race. We hadn't been going for long when, on rounding a bend, one of my wheels parted company with the car. Well, you can't do much about that, can you? The car left the track, rolled down a bank and was quite badly crashed, but again I escaped without a scratch and walked back to the grandstand. A bit upsetting this; after two years racing with no sign of an accident, two of them had to happen in three weeks. Even if my nerves weren't shaken, I must admit I began to wonder. Moreover, Jinx and Co. were not finished; they thought up something new for me in the next event which took place an hour or so later.

I was going along quite well. I had but small hopes of catching Rudolf Fischer on a Ferrari, since my H.W.M. was not quite fast enough for that, but it was able to hold off the rest of the field. Even so, I was lucky to finish second, because my fire extinguisher burst in the cockpit, spraying me with foam.

On and on it went, this bad luck period. I crossed over to the Isle of Man for the British Empire race, which I had won the previous year. My mount was a Frazer Nash, which was quite fast enough to give me a chance of winning; but no, this time the ignition system broke down, and after three or four pit stops to try to put matters right, I was forced to retire.

In an hour I had hopped into a plane for London and caught another for Monte Carlo and the Monaco Grand Prix. There were two races in the Principality, the first being called the G.P. de Monte Carlo and the other, more important, the G.P. de Monaco.

Here again I appeared to be going extremely well in the former event, and was able to ease off the engine of the Frazer Nash because it looked as if I had the race in my pocket. Then the studs holding the rear wheels broke and I had to retire.

Never mind, better luck in the senior event—so I thought. This time I drove a Jaguar, fast enough, given a straight race, to beat the foreign opposition, of which there was plenty. The race is held over 100 laps of a two-mile circuit and is known as the race of the one thousand corners—ten of them in each circuit. I took an early lead and kept going. At one point there was quite a large oil patch on the road, and Reg Parnell, just ahead of me—though a lap behind—skidded into a graceful pirouette which took him into the straw bales. A moment later my car took charge, and there was nothing to be done about it. I followed Reg Parnell into the "hay-wagon", as did other cars behind. Some of the drivers got bruised and scratched, but I was O.K., and so was the car. So I man-handled it back on the circuit, and began to overhaul the few that had passed me while in the straw—the car was going well when officials flagged me off the course. Why? Because enthusiastic spectators had helped me to push my car out of the straw on to the track again, and that entailed disqualification. Fair enough, and in strict accordance with racing rules, but we were a little peeved that the yellow warning flag to denote oil on the track had not been hoisted, so that we had driven on to the slippery patch without warning.

I hoped the gremlins on my back would decide by now that I had had my share of their attention, but they were not quite finished yet.

5

PORTRAIT OF A CHAMPION

I

My engagement with Jaguars had prevented me from driving one of the B.R.M.s which were racing at Albi. I was very sorry about this, but the international calendar had become so crowded that there was no way of avoiding the clashing of important events. Albi was very disappointing. The B.R.M.s showed their turn of speed all right, but again they were unreliable and could not finish the course, even though they had the great Fangio and his compatriot, Froilan Gonzales, at the wheel.

The two Argentinians had in fact roared away from the field. Gonzales, after a bad start, put in a record lap at 106 m.p.h. to get behind Fangio in second place. For about thirty miles the B.R.M. staggered everybody; then the trouble began, and it was not long before they were both out with engine trouble. The B.R.M. chief expressed himself as well satisfied, but the car was still a "potential" with a very blank and dismal record behind it. However, the news was flashed to me at Monte Carlo that it was intended to send two B.R.M.s across to Ireland for the International race and that the drivers would be Juan Fangio and Stirling Moss.

Superstitious thoughts began to run through my head. Here was I, completely in the doldrums with bad luck dogging me, and here was the B.R.M. which seemed to have its own particular brand of gremlin. Right, let's mix the hoodoo breeds and see if they'll exterminate each other. What a hope! Over to Ireland I went. I lasted five laps, and was then in the pits with incurable overheating trouble. Fangio did not stay in the race for long either, his trouble being with fuel supply. It was just about the last straw.

The long, patient optimism, the great support that had been given to a fine cause, turned to ridicule. By now, probably £250,000 had been spent on the B.R.M. project; tens of thousands of sympathetic enthusiasts had subscribed to the B.R.M. Supporters' Club; and it had all led to—what? Failure after forgiven failure and now, just jeers. The critics who had been generous in their excuses for the many failures, at last turned against the car which they had so jubilantly welcomed and so kindly defended. They asked for its complete withdrawal, since it was doing us harm. It was the generally held opinion, and more particularly abroad, that the B.R.M. was the brain child of the collective ability of the British industry; that it had been more or less sponsored by the Government to show the flag. Was this the best that could be produced by such concerted action? The general reaction of the public—and it was an immense public, not merely those interested in motor racing—could be summed up in the Biblical phraseology: "Shall I forgive my brother seventy times seven?"

I had thrown my lot in with the B.R.M., and would stick to the fallen idol, but it did seem that it was a bug-ridden failure and that nobody was able to get rid of the bugs. It was too late now for any real recovery to be made, because Formula 1, for which the car was built, was obviously on its way out, and all that remained were the few Formula Libre events in which it was not likely to meet any really formidable opposition. It was destined to take a place in the chorus with some elderly survivors of the pre-war period and a few privately owned cars. Was this to be the ignominious swan song on which so much money and enthusiasm had been lavished? Time would show.

The B.R.M. was being called the lame duck of the race

track. How vividly I recall the disconsolate Fangio sitting gloomily in the car while mechanics tried to diagnose the trouble; I did not know then that my association with the great Argentinian was to develop into a partnership which yielded a golden harvest of victories. I think, at that time, I was more depressed than I had been for some time. Nothing would go right; yet there was no real justification for my low spirits. After all, in but a few years I had been linked up with one of the world's greatest drivers and had so improved my own technique that I had become established. I am not much addicted to introspection, so that though I was unhappy over the long sequence of misfortune, it did not weigh too heavily on my mind. Indeed, the excitement of the next event always drowned any pessimism occasioned by the last.

II

It is opportune, I think, to tell you something about Juan Fangio, with whom, as I have said, I was later to race on most intimate terms.

Although a much older man than I am, he had started later in life but had a meteoric career to stardom. At first his reputation was confined to South America, and his first appearance in Europe did not give promise of his later triumphs. It was in 1948 when, with a long string of Argentinian victories behind him, he first came to Europe, a shortish, dark man with powerful shoulders and the clean, healthy look of an athlete. He could not speak a word of English and only a little Italian. He was content, in that year, to do little more than hold a watching brief over the leading Continental drivers, carefully noting their technique and occasionally racing an Italian Maserati or a French Simca without achieving anything outstanding. By the time he went back to his South American home, he had learned a great deal. He had seen the greats in action; he had admired the superb skill of Farina; and the next year he returned to Europe at the head of a racing stable of mechanics, ready to give challenge to the best European drivers. People began to sit up and take notice when he won the San Remo race, and they sat up a bit straighter when he beat the leading drivers, aboard factory-tuned cars, in five other events. Stories began to be told of this newcomer to the stars. It was said, for instance, that he had started as a bus-driver, which was only a half-truth, since he ran a motor-cycle firm in his native country and sold buses among other vehicles. He was Eva Perón's private chauffeur; another half-truth, in that though he may have driven the then Dictator's wife, his only real association with the Peróns was that he was a national hero and was supported strongly by the Argentine President in his quest for world honours.

Soon, Fangio became one of the most picturesque as well as the most successful of drivers. His vivid blue overalls, also worn by his mechanics; his retinue of reporters and broadcasters who followed him around so that news of his victories could be flashed across to his native land, combined to make his appearance anywhere a most colourful one. Juan Fangio had amalgamated the styles of other great drivers into one of his own. Calm, collected, yet with plenty of devil in him, he was a great exponent of the "drift". He was always fastest out of a bend, having discovered the art of pointing the car to the ensuing straight before he was fully round.

The mighty Alfa Romeo team, which was at that time carrying all before it, recognised in Fangio a valuable addition to their team, and signed him on. So he became a team mate of Farina, and in one of their first races he scored a great triumph. It was in the Monte Carlo Grand Prix. Farina dashed away with the lead, but soon had the unusual experience of being passed by another Alfa Romeo— Fangio's. At a bend on the sea front Fangio made a perfect turn. Farina, behind him, skidded into the wall, and so began a pile-up in which nearly a score of cars was involved. The pile-up eliminated all those who had any chance of catching the Argentinian, and Fangio won in a veritable canter—a very impressive curtain-raiser to his racing career with Alfas.

This race was followed by the complete domination of the European racing scene by the three F's—Fangio, Farina and Fagioli. Fangio in 1950 won seven major European events. Then came the great challenge of the Ferrari stable, which was successfully maintained until the Alfa Romeos retired from racing. It was during this great Alfa *v.* Ferrari duel that Fangio had an unusual experience. It was in the Belgian Grand Prix on the extremely fast Francorchamps circuit. Farina and Fangio had been tearing round at unprecedented speed, Fangio having smashed all records with a lap at over 120 miles. But the speed had taken heavy toll of the tyres, and at the half distance all the Alfa Romeos wanted their "shoes" mended.

Farina came in first, and after a quick change was away again. Then in came Fangio and sat patiently by while mechanics tried to change the rear wheels. One of them refused to budge. Not all the hammering and coaxing would shift it. Finally they had to remove the brakedrum and fit a new tube and cover to the rim. Was Fangio disconcerted? Well, if he was, he didn't show it. He calmly drank from a bottle, now and again pouring some of the beverage over the top of his head so as to cool himself off in the terrific heat. It was a long time before he could restart, and he was out of the hunt, but during the remainder of the race he showed what he really could do in an effort to get among the leaders again. With a superb demonstration of skilful driving which left the crowd gasping, he gradually overtook a number of cars, but could get no nearer than ninth. So this lion and lamb of a man occupied a lowly position after a great effort.

He is both lion and lamb because when the occasion demands he can roar round the track without regard for his car. To win, he will extract the utmost, getting from it every ounce of power, every yard of speed. Yet, when occasion permits, he will treat his car with gentle concern, nursing it, almost caressing it. For my money he is the greatest driver I have ever seen and his prowess can be a target for us all to aim at, although I doubt if anyone will reach his position in my lifetime.

III

Let me return to my tale of woe and the unfailing presence of those little gremlins. For a long while I picked up an occasional damson, but the plums continued to evade me. The next big event was Le Mans and the epic 24-Hour race. For me, it was disastrous. I was in the official Jaguar team, and hopes were high. I got off to a good start for, although seventeenth from the front when we sprinted across the road to start up our engines and get away, I had soon run into fourth place where I was comfortably placed after the first lap. But the Jaguars were, undoubtedly, a little too experimental that year, and within an hour or so the whole team was out of the race owing to overheating.

The German Mercedes, which for some time had threatened a return to road racing, ran off with all the honours, finishing first and second; but without belittling their performance, they were a little lucky, for the Frenchman Pierre Levegh had headed them off for 23 of the 24 hours, driving single-handed all the way. He led by 25 miles with just an hour to go when the engine of his Talbot failed. So another link was forged in the lengthening chain of bad luck.

One lesson my father taught me is that bad luck often results from mistakes of our own. Those Jaguars were specially prepared for the race, perhaps too specially. It was undoubtedly the fact that what was right in theory proved to be wrong in practice, so that the effect sprang from a deliberate cause, which cannot be attributed to bad luck. Levegh was regarded as "very unlucky", but the concrete fact is that he changed down instead of up, due of course to fatigue. As for me, personally, well it seemed that the off-setting tide had not reached the point where it would turn and carry me along on its flow. Le Mans was most disappointing, but with a full programme ahead of me, there was no reason, not even any time, to mope. This is easy to say, but at times, damned difficult to follow out.

Within a week I was engaged at Spa, Belgium for the Grand Prix of Europe, driving what the Press were pleased to call "the Mystery E.R.A.". It was in fact a special car bearing the historic name of the veteran cars that had done so well in previous years, but I was out almost as soon as I had started with a broken connecting-rod which locked the engine solid. The race was won easily by Alberto Ascari on a Ferrari, with the evergreen Farina second and Robert Manzon on a Gordini third; quite a triumph for the Continental cracks, but the real hero of the race was the new star Mike Hawthorn. It was his first appearance in a classic Grand Prix event, and the conditions were such as to unnerve the most experienced of drivers, with blinding rain pouring on a slippery course. For 300 miles he drove with the touch of a master, taking his Bristol Cooper into fourth place, although it had nothing like the speed of many he passed during the long and hazardous race. Even such a first-class driver as Ken Wharton got into a violent skid at 100 miles an hour, but fortunately crashed into some bushes, which, if they left a few thorns in him, at least formed a nice soft cushion to lessen the impact.

At last I parted with my gremlins. Over my shoulder went one care, and all the others followed suit. It was at the Rheims Grand Prix for sports cars, and I was at the wheel of a Jaguar fitted with the new disc brakes, the outcome of

(Above): Stirling at Silverstone in 1952, with the "G" type E.R.A., a car which he drove for a season but with which he had little success. *(Photo: T. C. March)*

(Below): At Silverstone with the 2½-litre Cooper Alta. The car was designed and built by Stirling, Ray Martin, the late John Cooper and Alf Francis. *(Photo: Autosport)*

(*Above*): Stirling in the Cooper Alta leading Tony Rolt in the London Trophy Race at Crystal Palace 1953, an event which Stirling subsequently won. (*Photo: N. W. Norman*)

(*Below*): With the Cooper Alta at Prestcott Hill Climb, 1953.

considerable research and experiment. It has become trite to say that a car is as fast as its brakes, but it is very true. It was a broiling summer day and when the race started the sun was absolutely sizzling. I had a dog fight with Robert Manzon for several laps, but it finished when the Frenchman skidded off the track, dashed between two trees and finally crashed into a pylon, the car being completely wrecked though Manzon escaped unhurt.

With his retirement, opposition practically disappeared. The Jaguar behaved perfectly, and for the full distance of 227 miles I was able to average the very high speed of over 98 miles an hour. Yet it was a close thing. As the race proceeded, I felt myself getting hotter and hotter. At the chequered flag I was only just able to bring the car to a stop and stumble out of the car, but what a moment it was for me! I remember that my father and Joe Sutton, my Jag. mechanic, rushed across to help me, since I was really groggy, but how inspiring to hear the strains of the British National Anthem and the mighty cheer which rose from the spectators! I believe it was the first time that our National Anthem had been played at the end of a Continental Grand Prix, and, believe me, it was a fine tonic. The serial story of failure was broken by the headlines: "Moss breaks the Hoodoo".

I was now due for a nominal change from motor racing—and I mean nominal, for though the Alpine Rally is, officially, a trial, it is as near to a road race as makes no difference. I was asked to skipper the No. 1 Sunbeam Talbot team in a strong representation by the British firm. As co-driver I had John Cutts, other couples in the team being Leslie Johnson and David Humphrey, and Mike Hawthorn and W. R. Chipperton.

Never were cars prepared with more thoroughness for the famous Alpine, nor plans more elaborately carried out. Our car was the same in which we had finished second to Allard in the Monte Carlo Rally, and they wrote of us as the spearhead of the strongest-ever British challenge. The event consists of a trial of 2,000 miles over the very roof of Europe with nearly all the journey on Alpine passes.

There were 100 starters from Marseilles, and just over a third of them were British. Six days later, a very small but select group of ten—five British, three French, one German and one Italian—finished the course at Cannes without loss of marks—and though we were one of the ten, it was only by the skin of our teeth. On the fourth day we had lost valuable time—35 minutes—in repairing a broken pipe from the exhaust manifold, and we knew it had to be very much of a Grand Prix race to Aix-les-Bains if we were to stay in the diminishing list of unpenalised drivers. We managed it, but it must have been a hair-raising experience for John Cutts, who stolidly and heroically sat at my side while I took risks in order to conform to the time schedule.

The casualties were heavy. As we dashed over the Alpine passes, we passed many stranded and some wrecked cars. Only 23 cars completed the course, and of these 12 were British. There were two outstanding heroes of the event. First, there was Ian Appleyard who, having won the coveted Alpine Cup for three successive years, was awarded a Gold Cup, the only recipient of that most difficult-to-win award. There was also Mike Hawthorn who, competing in his first Alpine, showed his ability to contend with every and any phase of high-speed motoring, by bringing in a second Coupe des Alpes for the Sunbeam team.

In a few days Mike and I were to oppose each other in another classic, the British Grand Prix Meeting at Silverstone. Considerable excitement was built up during practice for this event when the Argentinian, Froilan Gonzales, put up the fastest lap on the B.R.M., which was entered in the Formula Libre Race, at 98·48 miles an hour, being much faster than Ascari and Villoresi, the two leading Ferrari drivers. What a crowd-bringer that was! It looked as though a British crowd would at last be able to see the ill-starred B.R.M. vanquish the leading Continental teams in a Formula Libre race. But it was not to be. In the early stages of the race Gonzales crashed, though he had shown that the B.R.M., with its most intriguing snarl from the exhaust, was one of the fastest cars on the track.

Ken Wharton, driving the other B.R.M., was not so fast and the team manager waved him in and told Gonzales to undertake a voyage of recovery in the hope of catching the leaders. He made a valiant attempt. From fifth place, he began to overhaul the leaders, and with only two laps to go had run into third place, but then the gear-box packed up and yet again the B.R.M. was wheeled to its familiar resting-place among the discards.

The big event of the day was the Grand Prix—decided in the Formula 2 class—and it proved an easy thing for Alberto Ascari in a 2-litre Ferrari. In winning, he practically assured himself of retaining the World's Championship, which title he had won the previous year. Again Mike Hawthorn showed his great qualities by finishing third in his completely outpaced but eminently reliable Cooper Bristol.

My own contribution to the proceedings was to have a fairly easy win in the 500 c.c. curtain-raiser over 45 miles. It was a most successful day's racing with a crowd computed at 100,000, most of them, no doubt, attracted by the prospect of seeing the B.R.M.'s romp home. It didn't happen, but they put up a most promising show and dwindling hopes were rekindled.

I had to do a forced march to get to Namur for the 500 c.c. Belgian Grand Prix the next day. We clocked in all right and won our heat at nearly 77 miles an hour, but in the final the front suspension broke and left me stranded.

IV

Back again to England, or rather Wales, for the newly instituted Welsh Championship meeting at Fairwood near Swansea. Leap-frog is a fine athletic game for youngsters, but it is a bit dangerous with racing cars, as I learned at the first bend, known as the Devil's Elbow. Immediately ahead of me a car spun round and I had to take evasive action quickly. So did a gaggle of other cars, and before I could get clear, one of them had jumped over me, scratching my racing helmet and smashing the screen. The Kieft was badly damaged, and I was left without a mount for the final. It might have been a lot worse; an airborne car is quite a hefty piece of machinery and if it had done its leap-frogging an inch or two lower, it would have undoubtedly meant the "blood wagon" for me.

There followed a period of routine racing, with nothing very exciting about it; a win here and there and a journey to the dead car park now and again. It was fun, and I spent some of the summer in a caravan, which seemed to me to be an excellent way of touring from one race track to another. My commitments included contracts with the B.R.M. for Formula 1 events, the E.R.A. in Formula 2, the Kieft in Formula 3 and the Jaguar in the sports car division, but the end of my association with the B.R.M. was in sight.

Until now, I had confined myself to racing British cars and would have continued to do so had there been any which would have given me a real chance of winning the classic races, but after all, I was a professional racer, and the machinery wasn't up to it yet.

The Germans had taken no part in international racing since the war, but there were signs that they intended to break into the business in a big way and challenge Italian supremacy in the Grand Prix series and British leadership in the sports car division. Their pre-war record which, for many years, had given them the ascendancy over all comers was an indication of their thoroughness. If they entered the lists, it was certain that they would be in it with both feet and would be backed by solid organisation. German firms never leave anything to chance if they can avoid it, as witness their domination of the Grand Prix scene before the war.

The name of Neubauer, their team manager, was legendary and deservedly so; for he had schooled so many other top-notch drivers with the iron hand of management. He knew the game from A to Z. He is one of the wittiest men I've ever met after hours. He is thoughtful and has a big heart. All his drivers both respect and like him. It was certain that Germany would not make its bid for international honours unless satisfied that she could vanquish all opposition. Future events were to prove that I was right. The Germans, like the Assyrians of old, swooped down on the fold and won back their pre-war supremacy. But more of that anon. There was plenty to engage my present activities.

In early August, a big festival of motor sport was organised by the *Daily Mail* at Boreham, in Essex. The sport had caught on in England to such an extent that new tracks, nearly always round the outer periphery of discarded aerodromes, were springing up everywhere and newspaper support from various firms had provided the wherewithal for attractive prizes. An enormous crowd turned up at Boreham for a well-arranged mixed grill of racing.

I had a full plate with an E.R.A. in the Formula 1 and 2 races, a Jaguar C in the 100 miles sports car race and a Cooper Norton in the 500 c.c. ten lapper. In the 500 c.c. event I couldn't whip up my horses and had to be content with third place, but we had lots of fun and games in the sports car event. I had become quite adept at the sprint across the track which had come to be customary in sports car racing; I got away to a fine start and was able to set the pace—and a cracking pace it was—to the dashing Duncan Hamilton, also on a C type Jaguar. The weather was appalling, with always the imminent danger of the back of the car slewing round on the slippery track, but I managed to keep on an even keel and led to the finish. Mike Hawthorn, driving a Frazer Nash B.M.W. in the 2,000 c.c. class, had a terrific duel with Ken Wharton, but in the later stages was beaten by clutch slip. He was, however, to give the crowd a major thrill in the Formula 1 race. At the wheel of a 2-litre Cooper Bristol he hung on to the leader, Villoresi, who was driving a Ferrari twice the size of the British competitor. In spite of the rain and slippery track, Hawthorn kept in the Italian's slip-stream and finally snatched the lead. Here was a real sensation; a British Formula 2 car snaking past an Italian Formula 1, and all due to the fine driving of Mike Hawthorn. The greater power of the Italian finally told, but Mike finished second in front of a number of foreign Grand Prix cars. Hawthorn was undoubtedly the hero of that day's racing.

The Argentinian, Gonzales, was at the wheel of a B.R.M., and he crashed it at Hangar Corner, where earlier Ian Stewart, driving a Jaguar, had ploughed through the straw bales. When Gonzales crashed, Ken Wharton on the other B.R.M. was given the flat-out signal, but he was a lame duck; once again, the B.R.M., still the darling of the race crowds, failed.

Having picked up a first and record lap at Brands Hatch on August Bank Holiday, I dashed over to France to take my place in a team of drivers commissioned by Leslie Johnson to prove the speed and durability of the latest model Jaguar XK120. Co-drivers were Johnson himself, Hadley and Fairman, and between us we drove for a week at an average speed of over 100 miles an hour, which really was something for the Coventry manufacturers to crow about.

Next came an event at Goodwood, where the British Automobile Racing Club had put on something original in the form of a nine-hour race to finish at midnight. It was in fact a miniature Le Mans, and stemmed from the long-distance races which, before the war, the club, then known as the Junior Car Club, promoted at Brooklands. It turned out to be a failure; the crowd was disappointing and so was the racing. I was one of the Jaguar team, with Peter Walker as co-driver. In the other Jaguars were Tony Rolt and Duncan Hamilton, and Peter Whitehead and Ian Stewart. We started well enough, and were soon in line astern at the head of the field with the Aston Martins chasing us in fine style. Then things began to happen. First Peter Whitehead skidded on the wet track and clouted a particularly hard barrier, damaging his car so much that he could not continue. Then Tony Rolt's car decided to break an axle shaft, and there was I left alone with Peter Walker to hold off the snarling hounds which were at our heels.

We managed to stay them off, but with less than two hours to go we were in trouble. One of the rear axle locating arms had broken, and though mechanics worked at it, we lost over half an hour and had no chance of getting back into the lead, though we did put up a voyage of recovery which enabled us to finish in fourth place. At the start of the race it seemed an obvious Jaguar victory, but it was one of those bad days for the marque and we just couldn't do a thing about it. The race was won by Peter Collins, one of our really top-notch drivers, and Pat Griffiths at 75·42 miles an hour, and it was a very fine performance indeed to finish a couple of laps ahead of the Italian Ferrari which occupied second place.

Ah, well, it just goes to show. A few days ago, we had taken that Jaguar round Montlhery at a rate of knots, covering 10,000 miles at over 100 miles an hour, and now all three cars had been beaten in a relatively short race of nine hours. That is the racing game.

There was one very curious incident at that Goodwood meeting; one which reads more like a page from a "whodunnit". Jack Fairman, one of the party at Montlhery, was driving a big-engined Allard. During a practice lap they found the car behaving mysteriously, and they went in to examine. They found a piece of lead, some grass and fluff in the carburettor. How had it happened? The car had been left for an hour or so while the drivers had tea, but they noticed that the engine was hot when they returned to it, as though somebody had driven it. The mystery was never solved, but you can take it from me that these tricks do not take place in motor racing by deliberate intent. Racing is as clean as any sport, and I have never come across an incident where a competing car was deliberately tampered with. I've heard tales of sugar in the petrol, but the racing boys do not go around interfering with cars on whose behaviour depends the lives of the drivers.

On the contrary, there is a camaraderie of the race tracks which makes rival camps assistant to each other. Quite often a mechanic from one pit will go to the aid of those who, in an adjoining one, are in difficulties.

There have been isolated occasions when, on the track itself, a competitor has been slow to give way or has even deliberately baulked a pursuing competitor, but it is most unusual and it is part of the accepted ethics of the sport that you should in no way hinder the progress of a faster rival. At the same time, there are recognised tactics, such as slip-streaming and bluffing, as with false signals. Racing technique, yes, but no cheating.

The year 1952 wound up with a series of successes in the 500 c.c. class and a few record laps, but nothing outstanding in the higher divisions. One of these records was at Charterhall, but it didn't help me to win. I was, in fact, about to overtake another driver when he shed a wheel and I had to take to the grass to avoid him. Eric Brandon, always the opportunist, saw his chance and slipped by, so I had second place.

The year had been quite a success and it was crowned by the award of the Gold Star—the third in succession—by the British Racing Drivers' Club, though the new star, Mike Hawthorn, came very near to spoiling my hat-trick.

Most interesting of the autumn events was the Goodwood meeting, where I had another escape from disaster. I had got away to a fine start but somehow or other got mixed up with Dennis Poore's Connaught. It meant an uncontrolled spin round the track until I was brought up short by a barrier.

What made the meeting sensational was that the B.R.M.s finished first, second and third in the Goodwood Trophy race, with Gonzales, Parnell and Wharton finishing in that order. It is true that the opposition was not very strong and that the race was only over a short distance, but it was, I think, a little naughty of the papers to talk about the B.R.M. going out with its flag flying and singing a brave swan song.

Mention should be made of a rather remarkable marathon which, at the request of the Rootes Group, I undertook with Leslie Johnson, John Cutts and David Humphrey. The idea was to drive a standard Humber Super Snipe from Oslo to Portugal, travelling through fifteen countries in five days. It looked like what in racing parlance is called "a piece of cake", but it gave us thrills more varied and more exciting than is one's usual lot on the race track. There seemed to be black ice everywhere, and to conform to the schedule speed we had set meant keeping on the move all the time, ice or no ice. Sometimes the car took charge, but we managed to keep it from the deep ditches and road-side fences.

Snatching cat-naps as and where we could was mighty hard work. I particularly recall one seven-hour stretch in vile conditions when my tired eyes, peering through the headlights, picked out an American car upside down on a Swiss Alp. I think I must instinctively have driven a little more carefully after that, but my passengers didn't think so; they expressed the opinion, in forcible terms, that it was "hair raising". We covered 3,280 miles in under 90 hours, most of it through snow and ice at an average speed of 40 miles an hour. It really was a first-class show on the car's part because it was completely standard and quite a big fellow to handle on those appalling ice-bound roads.

Just before Christmas the British Racing Drivers' Club held its annual dinner. The Duke of Edinburgh presented me with the Gold Star and had some nice things to say about "dressing the shop window" by winning motor races. I learned at this social function that Mike Hawthorn had accepted an offer to join the Ferrari team as a regular member and was, indeed, on his way to the Argentine to fulfil winter engagements entered into by the Italian firm. He was to do extremely well and soon proved, in the best company, that he had every right to inclusion in the exclusive field of Grand Prix "works" drivers. Little did I think that I was to have an almighty battle with Mike for the title of Champion Driver of the World a few years later—which I was to lose by a single point!

It had not been a particularly good year for me so far as important successes were concerned, and I don't suppose I was much in pocket after the profit-and-loss account came to be reckoned up, but I had gained more experience. Incidentally my caravan was, after a little while, discarded. It broke loose and made a mess of itself at the bottom of a hill, down which it free-lanced after casting anchor from the back of the car. I decided that in future I would revert to hotel life during my Continental travels. There was no definite news from the Mercedes stable. I was quite content to carry on with the "bread-and-butter" schedule of racing round the aerodromes with occasional highlights such as the Monte Carlo Rally and the Alpine. Prospects were bright, because motor racing had taken a keen hold on the sport-loving public and crowds were increasing considerably. Indeed, to those of us whose services were in demand, the international calendar was quite crowded, to say nothing of the national events which took place every week-end.

6

CONQUEST OF THE DEMON

I

As usual, the New Year started with the Monte Carlo Rally, that annual battle of the nations which, more than any other event either on track or road, was the most unpredictable. There had been times when the weather conditions were so good that the trial was little more than a farce, and others, such as the last one, in which only a tiny percentage of the starters could reach the final check on the shore of the Monte harbour. The only thing you can do about it is to prepare for the worst and hope for the worst.

It so happened that the 1953 rally was easier than normal, though not for me personally. I was to drive a Sunbeam Talbot again with journalist John Cooper and Desmond Scannell as co-drivers, and our car had been entered for the team prize with G. Imhof's and Leslie Johnson's Sunbeams. When the party left for Monte Carlo which was to be our starting point, I remained in bed with a temperature, a particularly inopportune and strong influenza bug having got into me. I recovered in time to hurry after my companions and get to the starting point, but I felt very washed out when we actually began the 2,000 miles trip which was to bring us back to Monte Carlo.

Everything went well, however. Apart from a little fog in the Swiss Alps we met with no difficulties, but at Amsterdam I reported to the medical officer for treatment with an extremely sore throat, no doubt a legacy from the bout of influenza. We carried on and checked in at Monte Carlo on time, and qualified for the final stages of the rally. Finally, we finished sixth to lead home the Sunbeam Talbot trio as winners of the team prize. There were the usual protests from disgruntled competitors, but there never was a Monte without some sort of criticism being made about the special tests. The new year had started well enough.

It was a fine rally for British interests. The outright winner was Maurice Gatsonides, the well-known Dutch driver on a Ford Zephyr; the two team prizes went to Sunbeam Talbot and Jaguar, and Ian Appleyard, one of the Jaguar team, came home with an armful of trophies including those for the best British performance, the Public Schools Trophy, the British Trials' Drivers Association's Cup and the R.A.C. Challenge Cup. Ian Appleyard is the son-in-law of Sir William Lyons, the Jaguar chief, having married his daughter Pat, and ranks among the most eminent of rally and trials drivers. A fine-looking couple, they are always the centre of attraction, usually in their white Jaguar, which must have won its weight in trophies.

There is no doubt that the fine showing of British cars in such events as the Monte was helping to boost our export trade, especially in the United States, where quite a vogue for sports cars was developing. Realising this, Sir William Rootes, always a keen exponent of the need for "dollars for Britain", set about the task of producing a sports car, and so was evolved the new Alpine Sunbeam, a development from the Sunbeam Ninety which had done so well in the Alpine Rally.

His main objective was the American market, and by way of introduction he planned a really convincing demonstration. Sheila Van Damm and I were asked to "give it the works" on the long and straight stretch of road known as the Jabbeke Highway, a dual carriage-way which was originally built as the northern extremity of what was to have been a great Continental motor-way extending from the

Belgian coast to the Black Sea. This ambitious project had been interrupted by the war, but the Jabbeke section had come in very useful as a testing ground for record attempts.

At her first attempt Sheila put in a run which, officially timed, beat two miles a minute. We took the car to Montlhery, where Leslie Johnson covered over 111 miles an hour and I added a little makeweight by lapping at 116 m.p.h.

Meanwhile, a replica was being shown to the Press at the Rootes Showrooms in Piccadilly, and three others had already been sent across to the U.S.A. At that time they were the only five Alpines in existence, but they were the nucleus of the spirited sales drive in America. Sir William and Sir Reginald Rootes crossed the Atlantic to pilot this drive, and the car immediately began to earn the dollars for which it was built. Just to help matters along, the Rootes group was awarded the Dewar Trophy for the most outstanding technical and engineering achievement of the year, the award being based on the fact that G. Murray Frame, Mike Hawthorn and myself had won three Alpine Cups and the Manufacturers' Team Prize in last year's Alpine Trial.

II

An interesting interlude occurred in the early part of 1953 after the Monte Carlo Rally, when the *Sunday Express* asked me to test a number of cars and write about them. It was good fun and I thoroughly enjoyed driving and writing the series, but I was amused with some of the criticisms levelled against me. They are a guarantee against a swollen head. I quote from one of them, in a letter to the newspaper: "Stirling Moss has neither the experience nor the qualifications to report on modern, everyday cars. Surely that should be left to seasoned motorists who had cars before the war." Another reader suggested that I thought the Alpha and Omega of testing cars was to see how fast I could screech round corners. I'll pass the first

77

criticism as fair comment but, after all, when you are testing a car it is necessary to stress it beyond normal usage so as to discover what the margin of safety is. I am quite sure that my friends among the motoring correspondents don't test cars by perambulating around in normal fashion.

I found myself unable to fit the Royal Automobile Club's International Rally into my engagements, but it was a case of "it's that pair again", for Ian and Pat Appleyard, again in that famous white Jaguar of theirs, marched off with the premier award.

I had spent a very busy winter, not at the wheel, but at all sorts of social functions to which I had been invited. It was Coronation Year, and I found myself acting as judge at beauty competitions, and fancy-dress affairs, participating in all sorts of little gala performances and signing autographs. I was a little worried over recurrent throat trouble and quite gratefully accepted medical advice to take a complete rest and get all the sunshine I could, so I decided to go to the Bahamas and become a "convalescent" for a couple of weeks or so and get back in time for the start of the racing season. I shall never regret that most delightful break of sunlit escapism. It really did me a lot of good, and I came back looking for fresh worlds to conquer. There had been some idea of my joining the American sales drive and showing off the paces of the new Sunbeam Alpine in the United States, but some technical hitch or other occurred and so I was able to take a real rest cure.

As I have indicated before, you cannot indulge in the hectic pursuit of motor racing unless you are 100 per cent fit, both physically and mentally, and in the course of a busy racing season, when your mind and muscles are working at top pressure, a great deal of your strength is sapped. So with the Monte Carlo Rally behind and a period of comparative slackness ahead, the opportunity occurs for rebuilding the tissues and coming back to face the starting flag in a state of "*Mens sana in corpore sana*", which is one of the few chunks of Latin I remember from my school-boy days.

I had severed my connection with the Kieft Co., of which I was a director, and went off on my holiday free from any ties, other than those contracts into which I had entered for the next season's racing. But holidays are strange things. You start on them with the avowed intention of letting your mind be a complete blank; you enjoy two or three days in utter contentment and then you find your attention wandering back to the race tracks and longing to get back to them. I had a thoroughly good time in the Bahamas, but I suppose I was quite unable to throw off my mental restlessness. Sometimes I wonder if people in some jobs ever get a real holiday, though the failure completely to dissociate my mind from professional activities has never interfered with my capacity for enjoyment.

These medical johnnies know their onions all right, and though I wasn't greatly impressed by their talk about worn tissues and the need for a sort of revivalist campaign built on complete rest, I really was a bit worried when they declared that I might not be fit for racing during the forth-coming season. You can have all the distractions in the world: sunbathing, surf-riding, fishing, but at any rate, so it seems to me, the more you try to blank your mind, the more you create mental turbulence. I must admit that nowadays I find it easier to leave my racing worries and talk of other things.

III

Back at last and all set for the season, which opened with the Goodwood Easter meeting. But what a rotten opening to the season! For a start I fell off my motor scooter and damaged an arm; then, when I got to Goodwood, my car was not ready, so I could not fulfil my engagements in the several events for which I had entered. I did manage to get on the starting line for the Earl of March Trophy for 500 c.c. cars, but then found myself held up by a traffic block in the big field. By the time I had won clear, I had lost all chance of catching Alan Brown, and finished in third place.

The meeting was chiefly remarkable for another victory spurt by the reconditioned B.R.M. This car had been taken over by a new concern, with Mr. Alfred Owen at the head, and in spite of its past record it was to be persevered with in Formula Libre events. There were two cars engaged for the unrestricted race, one with Ken Wharton at the wheel and the other in the charge of Reg Parnell.

Among the opposition was Piero Taruffi in Mr. Tony Vandervell's Thinwall Special, a modified Ferrari which was to do well later on. There were also the ever-smiling Baron de Graffenried on a Maserati and a gaggle of E.R.A. and other old-timers. Ken Wharton jumped away with the lead and held it throughout, though Parnell was soon out of the hunt with supercharger trouble. Wharton put up a new record for the circuit at just over 92 miles an hour, and had the big crowd of spectators on their feet when he crossed the line an easy winner.

The following month the Mille Miglia came round again, and the big entry included the names of nearly all the great Grand Prix drivers. I drove a Jaguar. We went off from Brescia like a flash, and I thought that I must be well up in the vanguard. But my joy was shortlived. In less than 200 miles I was sitting disconsolately in a car whose rear axle suspension had given up the ghost. So 1953 was going to see a return of the gremlins, was it? Never mind, they'd sat on my shoulders before and had been shaken off.

British representation was strong with Jaguar, Healey and Aston Martins as the spearhead, but it came to be a case of the ten little nigger boys. Only Reg Parnell, on an Aston Martin, was able to achieve anything worth while, finishing fifth behind Gianni Marzotto, a very wealthy enthusiast

(*Right*): With the "D" type Jaguar on the Dundrod circuit, Northern Ireland, for the 1954 Tourist Trophy Race. Note how badly the front of the car has been pitted by stones flung up by the rear wheels of other competing cars.
(*Photo: Louis Klementaski Ltd.*)

(*Left*): Stirling driving a Grand Prix Mercedes-Benz at Monte Carlo, May 1955. The car was eventually forced to retire with an obscure mechanical defect.

(Above): At Sebring with Donald Healey and the Austin Healey 100S which Stirling and Lance Macklin brought home in 6th place in the 1955 Sebring 12-hour race. This car won the series production award.

(Below): Stirling driving the 1500 Porsche Spyder in the 9-hour race at Goodwood. Whilst leading the class by a handsome margin Stirling subsequently retired after colliding with Tony Crook when the latter lost control of his car on a patch of oil. *(Photo: Charles Dunn)*

(*Above*): The start of the 1955 Mille Miglia with Moss and Denis Jenkinson in the 300 SLR leaving the starting ramp. The number of the car also indicates the starting time; thus this photograph was taken at 7.22 a.m. (*Photo: Sport and General*)

(*Below*): The finish of the Mille Miglia. A jubilant crowd cheer Moss and Jenkinson to victory after their record drive.

(*Above*): The start of the 1955 British Grand Prix at Aintree, with Stirling driving Mercedes-Benz No. 12 and Fangio alongside driving No. 10. The race was subsequently won by Stirling. (*Photo by courtesy of Rootes*)

(*Below*): The maestro and the pupil. Stirling discusses a point with Juan Manuel Fangio, World Champion, and the man who could be said to have taught Stirling much of his track craft.

who set up a record average speed of 86 miles an hour. Marzotto had won in 1950 so his was no flash-in-the-pan triumph.

There is no other sport in which there is so sudden a drop from triumph to disaster. There you are, sitting at the wheel of your car with the engine humming rhythmically and well. The rear of a car gradually comes nearer to you as your greater speed closes the gap. The narrow road seems to close up to a mere path as you put your foot down; you pass, probably leaving in your wake a sportsman who has waved you on. The road ahead is uninterrupted; you go faster and faster until it seems that you are aiming the front of your car at an incredibly slim target. Now and again, the music of the wind changes into a swish as you pass through a village.

The miles are reeled off so that the kilometre stones look almost like gravestones, and still everything is as it should be, with your spirits buoyant and your hopes high. Then you hear, or feel, a jar somewhere in the rear, or your engine loses the smooth melody of its note and turns into a syncopated discord. Maybe you feel hot oil seeping on to your legs, or steam clouds rise from the bonnet. Any one of a number of things can happen, but they all mean the same— you are out.

All the months of preparation: the practising, the planning, the organisation, the expense, have succumbed to some trivial little thing which has developed into a major fault. You sit miserably in your lifeless car while competitors who earlier you had passed, roar by, not jubilant, not boastfully, but with a gesture of commiseration. When next they stop or slow down sufficiently to give a signal they will report that Moss is out, and even the rival camps will receive the news regretfully, so that when, eventually, you crawl into a control there is nothing but sympathy for you, and you know that the expressions of it are sincere. I think that we all—I know that I do—recover quickly from

such disappointments, accepting the situation with philoso-
phy and taking a vivid interest in the progress of those who
so lately were rivals. The incident is dismissed with the
thought that it will be your turn next.

Then came Silverstone, for the annual international
meeting and a big race programme for 500 c.c., production
and Formula 2 racing cars. I was down to drive in the
two production car events, one for touring and the other
for sports vehicles and the International Formula 2 race.
I nearly missed all of them. It happened on the first of
the two practice days. We were travelling very fast and I
was trying out the car to see what she really would do
after a few warming-up laps. The Jaguar certainly had a
turn of speed. She went like a bomb—but not for long. I
had just taken the mild but very difficult curve at Abbey
Corner and was in line for the straight ahead, when the back
of the car swung round. I was doing over 110 miles an hour,
and when the back of a heavyish car starts trying to beat the
front wheels, you are faced with an emergency. I wrestled
with the wheel, snaked her out of the skid after spinning
round and then—horror of horrors—a rear wheel struck a
soft verge, the car overturned and there was I, semi-conscious
but, as far as I can recall, in no acute pain.

Out came the "blood wagon" and back to the ambulance
station in the paddock I went. Dimly I saw the faces of
the crowd that had gathered round as I was lifted into the
emergency tent; strange, distorted faces that still were
familiar; shaky faces as though I were seeing them through
rippling water. A cursory, superficial examination and I
was packed off to Northampton Hospital. Nothing was
broken, just a few big bruises and shock. From this I soon
recovered and became a little fretful. How long must I
stay in hospital? I wasn't hurt, not badly, and felt quite
fit enough to get back to the track. I suppose I must still
have been a little dazed, but all the while I was ruefully
contemplating the decision of the doctor that he would

let me know later whether I was fit enough to drive on Saturday.

Saturday! What about tomorrow? A good night's rest and I should have completely recovered. But I did not have that good night's rest. I tossed and turned, dozing off at intervals and waking with that strange sense of unreality which comes to you in a strange bed, an unreality which soon focuses itself on the hard fact that you are in hospital. The next morning I felt quite well, with nothing more painful than the mental realisation of the fact that I had crashed, and the certain knowledge that I was not only fit enough to drive, but that to do so—and at speed—would do me more good than anything else.

Fortunately the doctor, even if he did not concur, expressed the opinion that there was nothing radically wrong with me. So, to everybody's surprise, I turned up for practice the next day and, believe me, it did my heart good to see how pleased everybody was; grins on the faces of the mechanics, joy expressed by the officials; it was an atmosphere which in itself was a first-class tonic. There was, of course, some little concern in the Jaguar camp. Was I quite sure I was all right? Don't you think you ought to take things easily for a bit? They brought out another car for me and as soon as I settled down in the cockpit I knew that I was not quite at home.

Near home, yes; but with somewhere at the back of my mind, that haunting, nameless dread, dismissed as soon as evoked, of Abbey Curve. I had always heard that the best thing to do after an air crash was to go up again; to master, before it had time to take root, any lasting impression that might settle into your mental make-up. All right, I would give Abbey Curve the works and show the corner that I was its master. But what was this? They stopped me as I was about to leave the paddock. The clerk of the course was not satisfied that I was fit to drive. True, the doctors at Northampton Hospital had given me the all-clear, but that wasn't good enough for the officials. They took me into the medical tent where I was carefully examined by Dr. Hopkins, the chief medical officer at Silverstone. The verdict was O.K. Off at last and there, approaching me, was Abbey Curve.

I knew the corner well and I knew exactly what I ought to do. Perhaps a more than usually long glance at the sweeping curve of the track, perhaps a flash of curiosity more than anything else. I was through the bend and I knew that I had taken it O.K. A song of triumph came to me; for half a dozen laps I sped the car round.

Whether it was sheer cussedness or some sort of reaction or other, I don't know, but I felt completely at home on the track and particularly Abbey Curve. No more would it have any terrors for me. Until the next time! What a strange, complex thing is the mind! Having applied the right remedy, I began to feel tired, as though I had wrestled successfully, though only after a hard fight, with the demons of imagination. Action was what I needed, so I took out the touring car for practice. At the end of practice I certainly was tired, but only with the healthy tiredness of muscular fatigue, for I had taken my medicine in large doses and had covered quite a number of laps.

Race day broke splendidly. I had slept well, and but for a few minor aches from my collection of bruises I was not only ready for the fray, but anxious to get into it. What a sight it was as I drove to the track. Wherever you looked there was a sea of faces. Probably it was the greatest crowd that had ever assembled at any motor race meeting in England.

My first engagement was in the Formula 2 race, in which I was driving a Cooper-Alta which, I knew, had not the pace of the Continental cars, but which was fast enough for me to "have a dip" at them. I managed to get off to a good start, but soon Baron de Graffenried had gone by me. Well, that was to be expected, but the Baron was a first-class driver and I elected to follow him closely. I did so. I haunted him all the way round the track and though his car was much the faster, he could not deny me the advantage of the slip-stream area behind him in which I was getting a first-class tow. There were the two of us, outstripping the rest of the field. I could not catch him; there was never any hope of it, but this was only the first heat of the Trophy race and I knew that if I could stay put there was nobody else in the field who could pass me, so I was all right for the final.

It turned out just like that. The Baron got his Maserati over the line first and there was I, like a little puppy on a leash, following him home in his slip-stream. We had both averaged over 90 miles an hour for fifteen laps, and that was quite fast going. The crowd was generous. They rose to us as we finished the race and I warmed to the appreciation they expressed. I had only finished second, but they yelled my name as though I had won.

Next came the Production Car race for touring vehicles, in which my mount was a Jaguar saloon. It was a Le Mans type start which, as I have described before, consists of running across the track at the drop of the flag, starting your "dead" engine and getting away. I had always been fairly good at this opening gambit, but it didn't look so good this time. After all, I was still a bit bruised, and not in real condition for a sprint over a track which always looks much wider than it is when you have to race across it. It may have been mind over matter, I don't know, but I was the first to get into the car after the trans-track sprint and with the engine starting up immediately I was away to a clear lead.

I was never headed. My car was the fastest in the race, and I was able to "take an easy", which was just as well. Leading from start to finish I ran out a comfortable winner, and again came that heartening cheer from the crowd. But so far as the day's racing was concerned, I had had it. In the Production Car race for sports cars, I just could not whip myself into winning form and could no no more than carry on, which I did, to finish seventh, with Mike Hawthorn driving a Ferrari, an easy winner. It was much the same in the final of the Formula 2 race. The Cooper-Alta went well enough, but I just wasn't on form, and it was lapping up petrol like a thirsty dog at a water-bowl, so that having managed to get into sixth place, delays for replenishments dropped me lower and lower.

There was a rather unusual incident in this race. Baron de Graffenried allowed his eagerness to overcome discretion, and beat the gun. It was no deliberate intent to gain an advantage; indeed, when he realised that he had crept over the line before the flag had dropped he braked and came to a standstill, but the stewards had no alternative but to dock him one minute for beating the starting signal. His pit attendants, no doubt smarting under the penalty, flagged him in after the race had been in progress for some time, but I think they made a mistake. The Baron was well in the vanguard, and even if the penalty had deprived him of victory, he probably would have finished well up.

To me it had been quite a satisfactory day's racing. I had won the Touring Cup race; I had proved to myself that I had suffered no ill effects from a crash which might well have had most serious consequences and that I was to live to fight another day. No occasion to grumble about your luck when you've been taken off the track in the "blood wagon" and come back the next day.

There followed a period of smaller races with a first at the Crystal Palace and another on the Nurburgring, both on 500 c.c. cars, and then I was ready for Le Mans, with Peter Walker as my co-driver in a Jaguar XK120 C. I couldn't have wished for a better "accomplice". Peter is a magnificent driver, one of those men who know all about the difference between daring and recklessness. He and I had just taken part in the Dutch Grand Prix, both in Connaughts which weren't anything like fast enough, but Pete had finished sixth to pip me by a place. I am sure if he had raced each week he would have been "a great".

But before Le Mans came round, there was an important race on the Dundrod circuit for the Ulster Trophy. There was not quite such an international field for this event, but there was Mike Hawthorn on a works Ferrari and Chiron on an O.S.C.A., formidable enough, especially the former. The home entry was excellent, and there were all the makings of a fast and exciting race. I had been asked to drive a Connaught, and when I got to Belfast I discovered that the whole city was talking about the great duel which was in prospect between Mike Hawthorn and Stirling Moss. No other aspect of the race was considered; all that mattered was that the two rivals, the youngsters who had broken into international racing, were to be matched against each other.

They were to be disappointed. The race was decided in two heats and a final, and Mike and I were in different heats. We had a real crack-a-jack race in my heat. I got away with the lead in the first lap with Duncan Hamilton as my nearest opponent. Then I had to call at the pits with gear-box trouble, spending half a minute there, which is a devil of a long time to make up. Back into the race I was lying sixth and had to undertake one of the voyages of recovery which are the sequel to any pit stop. Gradually I caught up. Duncan Hamilton, driving with his accustomed daring, was unlucky enough to hit a bank. He recovered and went on, but I whooped down the home straight with my foot hard on the floor. I was catching Duncan, but there was only a short distance left of the ten-lap race.

Fifth, fourth, third and at last second only to Duncan. I was lapping at just under 90 m.p.h., but though I espied the Hamilton H.M.W. now and again on the longer straights, I could not catch up with him and was finally beaten into second place by a matter of nine seconds, which wasn't so bad considering the pit stop.

Mike ran away with the second heat, winning it from

Ken Wharton, with the Irish newspaper owner, Robert Baird, putting up a first-class performance by finishing third. Now the crowd was really ripe for the final and the duel that they had so excitedly anticipated between Mike and myself. My car had been in the hands of the mechanics, but they had not been able to remedy the gear-box defect which had caused my first heat pit stop, so the Connaught team manager decided to let me drive Roy Salvadori's car. That suited me. But it was not to be.

The clerk of the course decided that we could not "swop horses" and that Salvadori would have to drive the car entered in his name. Technically, I think this was an error and I believe the clerk of the course told the entrant later that had he been given time he would have put the matter to the stewards of the race for a ruling. As it was, the loud-speakers blared out the fact that I would be a non-starter in the final, and so Mike and I never had our duel. I am not so sure they would have enjoyed it to the extent they had hoped, however. The Connaught was not really a match for the works Ferrari, and I should have had a really tough job to keep on terms with Mike.

But it was very disheartening, and I could do nothing but adopt the rôle of spectator and watch Hawthorn run right away from the field and win decisively from Ken Wharton. Mike was not to be envied, for the weather was atrocious and if his winning speed was appreciably less than that achieved in the two heats, it does not in any way detract from his achievement. You can't break records when your wheels are awash in flood water. A feature of the Connaughts' racing in Ulster was that they were equipped with fuel injection, as distinct from normal carburation, and it sometimes occurs that entries are made for events so that the sponsors can gain data which are available nowhere else than on the race track. This means that a firm showing up poorly in the results list could get more real value out of the event than the winner.

It has never been the fact that the dividend from racing is measured only in terms of prize money or trophies. Those of us who are just professional drivers, with no pretence to expert knowledge such as is possessed by the designers and the back-room boys, realise that it is sometimes our job to act as assistants to the experimental departments. Don't misunderstand me. The manufacturers are far too wise to jeopardise their chance of winning a classic race by testing out an experimental unit. The industry maintains a fine research station near Nuneaton where the worst of all road conditions are simulated, and it is only after thorough testing there that the race track is used to make assurance doubly sure. I must say, however, that I feel that MIRA, as the test place is called, should be open to racing-car manufacturers and owners.

Sometimes the results obtained under tests in the preliminary stages are not verified when it comes to the fiery baptism of racing. That is why you sometimes see a complete team of cars eliminated from a race; not because an experimental unit has failed, but because faith in a unit which had in fact passed through enough experiments to warrant installation in the racing car, has been misplaced. Some of the lesser races are used for trying out developments, but not usually the real classics. Racing cars are like babies which have their teething troubles and respond to treatment, but they grow into adolescence and eventually to maturity, and each phase has its own ailments. So the car in its first race is something of an adolescent. Not until it attains maturity of race-bred perfection does it become a real contender for honours.

The same may be said about drivers. A man may have all the qualities necessary to make a real champion, but he cannot become one until he has had vast experience. You cannot produce a star overnight; all you can do is to discover the material which might develop into the stuff of which champions are made.

89

7

BRITAIN TAKES THE LEAD

I

L E MANS, 1953, the scene and the occasion of the greatest triumph ever to have been scored by Britain in international motor racing; one which was to have resounding repercussions in the world market. It was, indeed, a famous victory and if Peter Walker and I played second fiddle to the magnificent performance of Tony Rolt and Duncan Hamilton, it was O.K. by us. Jaguars won. It will be recalled that in the previous year, the Jaguars, having won in 1951, had been a little too experimental and had gone out like a light in the early stages of the marathon with overheating. This year was to be very different.

Entry for the race was one of the strongest in its long history. The Italian Ferraris, Alfa Romeos and Lancias, the French Gordinis and Talbots, the American Cunninghams—biggest engined of all competitors—were there to give battle to the Jaguar team in which were Peter Walker and myself, Tony Rolt and Duncan Hamilton, and Ian Stewart and Peter Whitehead. All the Grand Prix cracks were in the race: Ascari, Villoresi, Trintignant, Marzotto, Louis Rosier: it was a terrific field, but lacking in the Mercedes representation, it being rumoured that the Germans were too busy preparing for next year's racing to give their attention to current events.

Practice times showed what was to come, for several of us had clocked in a circuit at over 100 miles an hour. Our

car was to take up position near the head of affairs and set
a fast pace. Villoresi in a Ferrari had a wrecking mission on
his hands. With a big-engined Ferrari he was detailed to
crack up the Jaguars. He did not succeed. For all his 4½
litres he could make no impression on us. Leader at the
end of the first lap was Sydney Allard, but he did not stay
there long. I passed him on the second circuit with a hoard
of foreign cars on my tail. In this I was assisted greatly by
something which might have been regarded as experimental
but which was in fact fantastic. Disc brakes; brakes that
bit into the speed as soon as you applied them and gave
much better service free from most vices. We stayed ahead;
for three hours our Jaguar was able to ward off the challenge of the Italian Ferraris, and the other two Jaguars were
close up, too.

Then minor derangements meant two or three stops at the
pits; not long ones, but enough to lose me the leading road
position. But Tony Rolt took over and resisted all efforts
to displace him. Sanesi, trying for another wrecking mission,
put up the remarkable record of 111·12 miles an hour in this
marvellous, almost unbelievable lap. Ascari had a crack at
Rolt, in the car he shared with Villoresi. No impression at
all; the three Jaguars, all fairly close together, roared around
at well over 100 miles an hour, and those who sought to break
them up were themselves broken and forced into retirement.

All through the long night, in the strange pattern of
ducking and jumping headlights, the British triumvirate piled
on the miles. Now and again there would be the sight of
a disabled car lying by the roadside; less often there were
the signs of a real crash. Dawn broke; still the Jaguars
maintained their positions, and the gallant fight of the Ferrari champions faded. They, and others who had tried to
stay in the hunt, were crippled by the unprecedented speed,
and the British train, with its three coaches, went on and on,
relentlessly, remorselessly. As must inevitably be the case in
such a long-distance event in which the cars ran faultlessly,

it became almost routine work with lap after lap being reeled off like numbers in an adding machine. There was little variation. The Jaguars were complete masters of the situation, and they remained so throughout the day which followed the uneventful night.

Finally, Rolt and Hamilton crossed the line with the colossal distance of 2,540 miles to their credit and an easy record speed of 105·86 miles an hour. It was the first time at which the Le Mans had been won at over 100 miles an hour. We followed behind with an average of 104·63, and then came Phil Walters and John Fitch on the giant American Cunningham. A magnificent achievement. They had split the Jaguar team, but Stewart and Whitehead came in fourth, only fractionally behind the Americans, to give the British team first, second and fourth finishing positions in the most hotly contested marathon and the most amazing day-and-night chase ever recorded.

The French were wild with enthusiasm. They forgot all about their well-beaten Gordinis; they forgot everything, in fact, except their delight at the stupendous performance put up by the British team. It was Coronation year, and there were demands for the famous Le Sarthe circuit to be re-christened and called the Elizabeth circuit. There were shouts of Elizabeth, Everest, Jaguar—Everest had recently been conquered and the emotional French just couldn't help linking the three great events of the year.

In what a remarkable manner the Jaguar had wiped out the sting of its humiliation in the preceding year! It was an occasion for celebration and celebrations were made not only at the finish of the race, but later, in England. The cars themselves were garlanded, like winning horses in a May Day procession, at a celebration at Coventry. The news of the victory was flashed all round the world, and the propagandist value of that three-pointed triumph to British export interests was incalculable. What consolation for those of us who had perhaps come to be a little despondent because of the bad runs which must come to all racing men! What heroes were Tony Rolt and Duncan Hamilton, two really top-notch drivers in their late thirties who forged another link to bind their racing partnership! Each had had fine war records, each had become godfather to the other's child and now they had shared the wheel in the greatest British victory ever achieved on the motor-race track. Do you wonder that we celebrated? Tony and Duncan paid high tribute to a great car.

And, of course, they were right, because no car ever had won through a more prolonged period of speed and endurance, but a single mistake by either of them would have made all the difference between success and failure. It was a long while before the acclamations of the Press died down; the time will never come when that epic team performance will be forgotten.

Whatever the rest of the season had in store for me, I would have no cause for complaint.

II

After the Le Mans affair came the Empire Trophy race in the Isle of Man. This was run under handicap conditions in accordance with engine capacity. The Manx course was short, twisty and had much of the "round-the-houses" element about it. I had a C type Jaguar, but it was not really suited to the circuit. My top speed was determined by the nature of the course rather than the power of my engine; I managed to finish fourth behind the record-breaking Ken Wharton who won on a Frazer Nash. So back I went to foreign parts for a dip at the Rouen Grand Prix.

Nothing doing. My Cooper-Alta wasn't in the same street as the Continental G.P. cars. Dr. Guiseppe Farina, who, though he did not know it, had set the model on which I fashioned my driving, won from Mike Hawthorn, and I came lumbering up among the chorus in tenth position.

Better luck in the twelve-hour sports car race which pre-ceded the French Grand Prix and was called the Rheims Grand Prix.

Jaguars had decided to rest on the Le Mans laurels and cut out the race, but this did not prevent me from borrowing a car. So, with Peter Whitehead as co-driver, we had a go at the "Champagne" stakes. Ferraris were out for vengeance and had entered a strong team, but, unlike the Manx course, the Rheims circuit suited us. Jean Behra went off at a rattling pace and led the Ferraris on the first lap, but was soon overtaken, while we tootled along very nicely, well among the leaders.

Race tactics, in a long-distance event, are determined by what the other competitors are doing. It looked as though the Ferrari and Gordini camps were out to engage in a wrecking expedition, and thundering close behind them was the American Cunningham. Between them they were col-lecting records at almost every lap, but Pete and I stayed put behind the three leaders with power in hand, waiting on the drama ahead of us. We were all set to move up when the time came. After four hours, a third of the race, Maglioli was well away with his Ferrari; the Cunningham was lying second and the Gordini third.

Carini, co-driver to Maglioli, asked for trouble when, despite warnings from officials who had laid it down that headlights must be kept on until 5 a.m., he went round lap after lap without them. Then, in the pits, he broke regula-tions again by employing more than the stipulated number of mechanics. The French officials promptly disqualified him —they had no option—though the Italians were furious about it. We were now in third place and "sitting pretty". Fitch went off the road in the Cunningham, then the Gordini limped into the dead car park to give us the lead. Thereafter, it was a mere procession. At the half dis-tance we were two laps to the good, and with nobody near enough to put up a challenge, we just went along on a tight rein, saving our horses for reliability's sake. Even so, we averaged over 105 miles an hour, a speed almost identical with Rolt and Hamilton's in the Le Mans race. It was another fine demonstration of British supremacy in the sports car field. It was followed by the French Grand Prix, and in this Mike Hawthorn achieved not only his greatest personal triumph, but a long-delayed victory for Britain.

Thirty years ago, the late H. O. D. Segrave had won the French Grand Prix, but no Britisher had done it since. Mike did, and to do it he had to beat such superb drivers as Juan Fangio, Froilan Gonzales, Guiseppe Farina and Alberto Ascari. Gonzales had a very fast Maserati and he jumped into the lead with Hawthorn, Fangio and Farina bunched together behind. At the half distance Gonzales went into the pits for refuelling, and this cost him 29 seconds, but contrary to the South American's expectations the Ferrari drivers made no such stop, and so they jumped into the lead with Fangio on a Maserati to give them battle. And what a battle it was! There was the British youngster ranged against the great Fangio in a car of approximately the same speed. They passed and repassed each other.

It must have been a big surprise to Fangio to discover that this newcomer, this relative upstart, could not only stay with him but actually pass him. They went round on the last of the 60 laps—312 miles—almost bonnet to bonnet with the crowds screaming in almost hysterical excitement. Round the bend to the final straight. You could not tell which of them was ahead, but the Ferrari bonnet was sticking out in front of the Maserati and when they crossed the line, Mike had won; we went mad, it was the most terrific win.

Poor Gonzales, driving like a madman, picked up most of the time he had lost by his pit stop and finished almost on top of Fangio while Ascari was only a few seconds behind. It was the closest, tensest Grand Prix race for many years and the finishing order is something Mike ought to frame. It read:

95

1st, Mike Hawthorn (Ferrari); 2nd, J. M. Fangio (Maserati); 3rd, J. F. Gonzales (Maserati); 4th, A. Ascari (Ferrari); 5th, G. Farina (Ferrari); 6th, L. Villoresi (Ferrari). Nobody had ever seen a finishing list like that, with a young Englishman's name ahead of the most famous names among all the Continental Grand Prix aces.

You see, it was not as though the European champions had been beaten by mechanical trouble. They all finished; none of them had had any trouble throughout the race, but they all finished behind our man though they had harried and challenged him from start to finish. Mike's performance on that day goes down as just about the greatest achievement by a Briton since the beginning of racing time.

We were showing the flag with a vengeance. We might not have the cars to challenge the Continent in the Grand Prix series, but I think we could fairly say that we had the drivers to match up against these men who in their respective countries were national heroes. Only Mike had so far had the opportunity of getting the same experience as them. Only he had a permanent place in a first-class racing team, and he had shown, in one short season, that he was a match for anybody. Neither were Mike and I the only pebbles on the beach; there were quite a number of magnificent drivers at home, such as Peter Collins, Ken Wharton, Peter Whitehead, Tony Rolt and so on. I could name at least another half-dozen, bang up to Grand Prix racing if only they had the cars or the experience. As a result of private enterprise, we were beginning to nibble at the game.

Alfred Owen and Tony Vandervell were spending bags of gold in an all-out attempt to produce a British G.P. car, but they were fighting an uphill battle against the supported and publicly acclaimed activities of the Italian and French firms. There never was a better case of the Churchillian statement "Give us the tools and we'll finish the job". There was ample proof of it, too. We might not be able to produce the specialised Grand Prix cars, but when it came to produc-

(*Above*): The finish of the 1955 British Grand Prix; an historic moment with Moss winning from Fangio literally by feet. This was the first time a British driver had won this event. (*Photo: Charles Dunn*)

(*Below*): Driving George Houel's 300 SL Mercedes-Benz in the 1956 Tour de France in which he was placed third. This shot was taken during one of the speed tests on the Rouen circuit, scene of the 1957 Grand Prix of France.

(*Above*): Close-up of Moss the driver concentrating at the start of the *Daily Herald* International Trophy Race, Oulton Park, 1956. He won this race driving an Aston Martin.

(*Below*): Moss the master in the wet at the *Daily Herald* International Trophy Race. He lapped all but the second man, Tony Brooks, before the event finished. (*Photo: Charles Dunn*)

tion models we were on top of the world. Le Mans proved it, Rheims proved it. The Continental countries were able to call on their top-notch drivers for these events, but they could not lower the colours of the British "Similar-to-what-you-can-buy" cars.

III

Soon we were able to give another demonstration of British supremacy, for after Rheims, we made our way to Marseilles for the Alpine Rally, that fantastic trial over 2,000 miles including over thirty mountain passes. This event is not a race, at least not on the international calendar, but it is more than an imitation of one. My very able co-equipier was to be John Cutts, a man of vast Rally experience. What you do is to get along as quickly as you can on the relatively easy stretches so that when you come to those rather frightening passes, where a single mistake can send you over the edge of the road to the valley thousands of feet below, you can reduce the risk.

Just to make things a bit more difficult, the promoters had put in a surprise "Alp" after the itinerary had been published, this being the Gavia Pass between Bormio and Ponte di Legno. Having reached St. Moritz without losing a mark and so still being in the running for an Alpine Cup, I decided to take full advantage of the day's rest which the programme allowed; however I didn't get it. The Italians, excitedly, gave us lurid descriptions of the Gavia, declaring it to be too dangerous to negotiate at the average set us. This wanted looking into, so instead of getting in a few hours "kip", some of us borrowed a car and went off to look over the run. The Italians had asked the British competitors to join them in a protest about the inclusion of the pass, but we weren't keen on this.

If the organisers had decided that the pass would constitute an eliminator, that was all right by us. Anyway, a little party of British competitors set off to survey the pass. It was a teaser! A rutty, narrow little road, well described by one of the party as a "goat track", wound up through the Alps, one stretch of it being a mere ledge carved out of a forbidding and nerve-destroying precipice. It was so dangerous as to be safe, if you can appreciate the paradox. What I mean is that, unless you were crazy, you couldn't go fast enough to hurt yourself.

When we came back, we told our colleagues all about it, and the whole British contingent decided to get to it as quickly as possible so as not to have to rush matters when we got there. Two or three cars overdid it and crashed on the way, but John and I arrived with time in hand and essayed the pass. On the ledge of the precipice the pass was blocked. One car, in trying to pass another, had run into it and there they were, locked in a most unfond embrace. There was nothing for it but to manhandle the cars and leave sufficient space to get by. That is what we did, but it took us precious time and we had to make it up. But not on that treacherous section. Discretion was definitely the better part of valour, and it was not until we got into the relatively easy section after the pass that it was possible to put up one's speed.

Even then it meant slithering on loose roads, with the choice of either taking risks and keeping up with the time schedule or playing for safety and losing the Alpine Cup. We chose the former, and finished the trial unpenalised. So did seven other British competitors, so that of the 25 cups awarded, we took a third. Among the four cup-winning Sunbeam drivers was that remarkable woman driver, Miss Sheila Van Damm. Sheila is not only a good driver, but a good sport as well. She is always cheery and very well liked in motoring, but don't let me mislead you. Sheila really gets a move on. When we checked in after the Gavia I turned to John and said, "Do you think Sheila can do it," because it had been really tough. Practically as I said this, a hooter blared and a Sunbeam Talbot came sliding round the corner and checked in; it was an elated Miss Van Damm. One of the greatest women drivers of all time.

Back to the race track for the British Grand Prix meeting at Silverstone and a nice comfortable drive in the 500 c.c. race by comparison. The Grand Prix itself was a superb race, with a terrific scrap between Alberto Ascari on a Ferrari and the man who was to succeed him as title-holder, Juan Fangio, on a Maserati. They finished first and second, with Farina third and Gonzales fourth. Notice how these great names kept figuring at the top of the awards list in the classic events. Gonzales was again unlucky, for he was delayed by an oil leak and couldn't get up with the leaders after the delay it caused him. Unluckier still was Mike Hawthorn, for he skidded on one of the oil patches left on the track by Gonzales, did a prolonged waltz round the track in his spinning car and finally biffed his tail into a boundary post. He was lucky to get out of it, since he started spinning at nearly 100 miles an hour, but he showed his tenacity by doing a bit of panel bashing and carrying on to finish in fifth place.

In the Formula Libre race, Fangio and Ken Wharton each drove a B.R.M., but though they finished second and third, the car did not do any good to its dismal reputation by finishing behind the Thinwall Special on which Farina won, incidentally putting up a lap record of over 100 miles an hour.

8

THE HOODOO RETURNS

I

AFTER a brief week-end at home, I flew to Lisbon for the Portuguese Grand Prix, as the prelude for about a month's engagements on the Continent. A spear I was carrying caused a lot of amusement, for I wanted to underwater fish, and hoped to get in a few brief spells in the Mediterranean between races. It is great fun swimming around in quest of elusive fish and sometimes you come across one which is more inquisitive than elusive—the poor fish. I might say it needs to be quite inquisitive if I am to get it!

It wasn't a very successful month. I managed to finish second in the Portuguese race in a Jaguar, but was quite outpaced by Felice Bonetto on an Italian Lancia.

Meanwhile, Mike Hawthorn was winning the Belgian 24-Hour race at Francorchamps, and I was in some sort of indirect trouble. It appeared that the Jaguar people had indicated their intention of competing in this event, and that I was to be one of the drivers. The Royal Automobile Club of Belgium apparently regarded this intimation of an entry as an actual fact, and when Jags. decided not to run they were reported to the International Federation for breach of contract. The Federation rules declare that entrants who deliberately refrain from running in a race may be disqualified for the rest of the season, and the rule applies to drivers as well as entrants. It didn't sound too good to me, but explanations were accepted and the matter was smoothed over, so I was not excommunicated.

The next big event on the programme was the German Grand Prix which, this year, was also the Grand Prix de l'Europe. I had the chance to compete in a new Cooper into which an Alta engine was to be installed. As is so often the case when a car is being put together for a race, all sorts of snags occurred, and it looked as though we should have to give up all idea of competing. But for twelve days and nights my crew of mechanics stuck to the job of preparing the car and we shipped it over to the Nurburgring with bits and pieces still waiting to be fitted. Not until the Friday morning did we get it across the Channel, and when we reached our destination the car looked more like a lot of spare parts than a complete entity. Indeed, a German official asked where my car was, and when we pointed to the "thing" he was speechless with astonishment.

The car wasn't really fit to race, developing gear trouble as soon as it started, so I found myself following the Italian drivers round that many-cornered course to finish sixth. In the vanguard most of the time was the "old gang" of Farina, Fangio, Ascari, Hawthorn, all four of whom once came very near to an unholy crash. After three of the 18 laps, Ascari was just ahead of the other three when one of his rear wheels parted company with the car. It soared into the air, but luckily shot over the heads of the tightly packed drivers following Ascari, whose car was running on three wheels and a brakedrum, and overshot the pits by 100 yards; a new wheel was soon fitted and he smashed the lap record in a desperate and most spectacular effort to get back among the leaders. He couldn't do it. Farina on the Ferrari and Fangio on a Maserati were first and second, with Mike Hawthorn a very fine third, despite the fact that in the later stages of the race his car had begun to lose some of its horses.

I returned from the Continent with very little in the kitty, but this was hardly surprising. You cannot match up an experimental car against the proved thoroughbreds of experienced racing stables when, even if your own car does not get mechanical troubles, it is still considerably slower. The race may not always be to the swift, but in an event including a dozen hares it is odds on one of the hares winning with the tortoise coming along behind.

I had a three-race engagement at a mammoth meeting on the Charterhall track in Berwickshire, and in the most important of them I managed to hold third place behind Farina on the Thinwall and Wharton on the B.R.M. until mechanical trouble took me out of the running. It wasn't long before Farina too was out, and the B.R.M. was left to win easily. Then, in the sports car race, things seemed well set for a win when an oil-pipe burst and that was that. It was a case of third time lucky, for I was first in the 500 c.c. race.

By now I was becoming ambitious for something bigger than baby class, and cocked my eye at the Goodwood Nine-Hour race, with an attractive first prize of £650 for the winner.

The race started at three o'clock in the afternoon, and the winner was the one who, by midnight, had completed the greatest distance. It looked like being another Le Mans, with Jaguars dominating the race, and so it was—for eight hours. Peter Walker and I set a cracking pace and held on to the lead for hour after hour, with Tony Rolt and Duncan Hamilton in second place. At about the half distance I was signalled to take it easy. I was able to do this and still retain the leadership. We reeled off the laps, almost monotonously, with nary a sign of anything untoward happening, but with not more than an hour to go the oil pressure went down, and the poor starved engine couldn't carry on. Most annoying after eight hours of regular running!

This left Rolt and Hamilton in the lead, but not for long; their car developed the same trouble and had to come into the pits. Goodwood is a shortish track, and one is always turning right. I don't think it quite suited the Jaguars. The disc brakes were red-hot at times, but as I have already said, the prizes are not the only harvest of the race track.

The Jag. engineers learned quite a lot about disc brakes as a result of that race, and the problem of keeping them cool engaged immediate attention, as well as oil surge remedies.

II

It was now autumn and the only remaining chance of scoring a major success was in the Tourist Trophy race on the Dundrod circuit. Again my chances appeared to be rosy. With Peter Walker as co-driver, I started with the assured knowledge that our car had superior speed to anybody else in the race. I had put up the fastest practice time, and had also established the fact that the road surface, with its rough top dressing, was going to be very hard on tyres. After a quick getaway I had the circuit to myself with the rest of the field strung out behind. I was "clocked" at 138 miles an hour on the flying kilometre, but just as I was settling down to it, the bonnet broke loose and I had to go into the pits for improvised repairs. Back again with the car overhauling the field rapidly, and then tyre trouble started.

We seemed to be doing nothing but stopping at the pits for more tyres; actually we had to stop at the end of approximately every ten laps on a circuit only $7\frac{1}{2}$ miles long. Still we managed to keep up among the leaders until the 107th of the 108 laps, when mechanical trouble put an end to the heartbreaking stops and sprints. At that time Jaguars were lying second to Ferraris in the World's Sports Car Championship, being two points behind. There was no point in going over the line into the "dead" park, so I stopped a few yards in front of the line and waited. I realised that once the chequered flag was down I could cross and be an official finisher, so when Peter Collins finished, I just pushed the car over the line to take fourth place, but with the third highest distance to my credit.

The event was run on handicap so that the third car to

finish, Ken Wharton's Frazer Nash, had credit laps and did not cover as many miles as my Jaguar. That meant four points in the Championship series and that put the Jaguar two points ahead, instead of two points behind the Ferrari. Unfortunately, the lead was not consolidated at the decider, which was the famous Pan American race, because Jaguars were not officially represented and the Italian firm notched the points necessary to win.

The rest of the season was almost barren of trophies or prize money, and it finished on a bad note when I broke my collar-bone at Castle Combe. I had won my heat in the 500 c.c. race quite convincingly, but was destined not to figure in the final. In the Formula 2 event I drove a Cooper 1100, and Tony Rolt a Connaught; we clouted each other rounding Quarry Corner. My lighter car got the worst of the impact, and started somersaulting. I found myself upside down in the car, and in a split second was topside again. The second somersault sent me flying out, and I cannot help thinking that my crash helmet saved me from disaster. As it was, in addition to the collar-bone, I damaged an arm and twisted a knee, so it was me for the "blood wagon" again to spend some hours in hospital at Bristol.

That incident again showed me the extraordinary manner in which instinct comes to the rescue. I have no clear recollection of my actions, but apparently I picked myself up and ran away from the track before finally collapsing. After a short while I came back to London and had a check-up at St. Thomas's Hospital. My arm, although completely broken at the shoulder was removed from plaster and Dr. Philip Bauwens used physiotherapy for its rehabilitation. I drove my Mk 7, fitted with a Borg Warner automatic transmission admittedly five days later, and in twelve weeks my break was completely mended and the muscle restored! I had hoped to be well enough to drive at Snetterton, the East Anglian course, but had not recovered sufficiently and had to content myself with the rôle of spectator.

It had not been a very good season for me, though I suppose I must have had my share of successes. I had done well in the sports car and 500 c.c. events, but everything seemed to be so unsettled in the Grand Prix field. The B.R.M. was "out of bounds" because it did not conform to the formula now used for G.P. racing. It really looked as if I should have to link up with one of the big Continental firms if I were to have any chance of meeting the famous Italian, French and Argentine drivers on level terms.

Patience, Stirling, patience; there's a good time coming!

III

The close of the year saw me on my way to America, with a view to examining the Pan-American course, having ideas of more active participation in the future. Actually, while surveying the course with Mr. "Lofty" England, the competitions chief of Jaguar, we had a minor accident when a stone was run over, but neither of us was injured. The Pan-American course is very fast at the finish and slow early on and very interesting, but it is nothing like as dangerous as we had been led to suppose. I reckon the Mille Miglia is far more dangerous.

The Pan-American course stretches from South Mexico to the U.S. border, and its chief danger lies in the long, straight stretches on which cars can be driven at their maximum. Speeds of 180 miles an hour should be quite possible on some of these stretches. There are, however, curious road conditions which change all along the route. There are no recognised pits, so that it is necessary to organise convoys of mechanics to follow the drivers whom they serve. This means a great deal of planning, with mechanics dashing off overnight so as to reach the day's destination in time to service the cars when they arrive.

What one might call the extraneous conditions are rather similar on the Pan-American circuit to those on the Italian

Mille Miglia course, in that—in their excitable enthusiasm—
—the spectators jeopardise their own lives and those of the
drivers by encroaching on the track. When you are concentrating on the road ahead in a race of this nature, it is most
disconcerting to have your attention distracted by the crowd.
A man may step out on to the road so as to get a view of
approaching cars and feel quite safe, but in doing so he
diverts the driver's attention and may cause him to make a
mistake leading to disastrous consequences.

After Mexico, I flew across the United States, enjoying the
superb hospitality which is characteristic of the Americans
and was delighted to see proof positive of the popularity of
our products, particularly in California. It would seem that
the Americans have rather neglected the sports car, being
more concerned with large and high-powered vehicles.
Whereas at home there have been British sports cars since
the inception of the industry; and in the fifty years or so that
have passed, we have improved the type. It is often stated
that the Americans are ahead of us in car design, but that
is only true of a particular kind of car; that is, the American
type. Where they have employed big capacity engines, we
have leaned towards the development of high efficiency from
small capacity.

It was probably the M.G. which pioneered the popularity
of the British sports car in the United States. Americans
regarded it as cute, and they were quite astounded by its
acceleration and speed. They liked its low rakish lines.
When the XK Jaguar came along it caused an absolute
furore. It was just what the doctor ordered for the film
stars of Hollywood, and they took the medicine with relish.
Another British car which quickly jumped into popularity
was the Triumph TR2, and at a time when a big dollar harvest was essential to the economic welfare of the country,
the British Midlands did more than its share of reaping it.

Having paid, literally, a flying visit to the United States
and gathered some useful data as to racing and commercial

conditions, I was back in England for Christmas, ready to plan my next year's engagements.

Ken Gregory, a devotee of 500 c.c. racing, was my manager. Young and enthusiastic, he knew quite a lot about the racing game. We had discussed plans for 1954 and had tentatively arranged that my best plan would be for me to acquire my own G.P. car, and free-lance. I liked the idea. It meant that I would do the racing and Ken would do all the thousand and one things necessary for organising and maintaining the programme. Possession of a G.P. car would not tie me down exclusively to any one firm, so that I should be free to race in Formula Libre, sports car and 500 c.c. events.

The surprise that awaited when I returned home was quite something. Ken had bought a "straight-from-the-stable" Grand Prix Maserati, one of the Italian cars with lots of power and a sleek body which placed it among the most handsome of top-class racers. But would it stand up to the Ferraris and the roaring pursuit of classic victories? Worse than this; I was really to be put to the test. Before I had had a slower car, and it's always easy to show up well in an inferior car because everyone is for the underdog. I was really worried. Time alone would show. I knew nothing about the Maserati until I was on the boat for England.

Until now I had raced British cars exclusively, and nothing would have induced me to change my mind except the all important one that I regarded it as extremely unlikely that any home product stood even an outside chance of winning a Grand Prix race. There were "potentials", but a professional driver, like a professional jockey, can only live on winners. After the past disappointing and rather unlucky year I just couldn't afford to have another one like it. The Press treated my decision generously, realising that I had relinquished hope of driving a British car to a classic victory and pointing out that I had not "sold" myself to the Italian firm, but had bought a car which would be raced in British green and not Italian red.

9

DRIFTING TO VICTORY

I

THERE I was, then, all set for the 1954 season, with my Maserati for Grand Prix racing, an agreement with Jaguars for sports car contests and a Cooper for 500 c.c. races. Thus equipped, I was obviously in for a very busy season and looked forward to making a voyage of recovery from the 1953 doldrums. It is not to be thought that those who are regarded as star performers by the public are indifferent to the plaudits of the populace. It is our bread and butter, and we must for ever strive to enjoy it. It is easy to slide. Every year the public is invited to choose the first dozen sportsmen of the year. In 1952 I was placed fifth behind Randolph Turpin (boxer); Geoff Duke (racing motorcyclist); Len Hutton (cricket) and Colonel Llewellyn (equestrian); but in 1953 I wasn't in the first dozen.

To fill up a crowded racing season, there were such events as the Monte Carlo Rally and the Alpine trial, so you can see that my engagement book hadn't many blanks for the coming year.

Just around Christmas, a newspaper asked a number of "celebrities", as it called them, to let its readers know what their New Year's resolution was to be. I had all sorts of grandiloquent ideas: "To win a Grand Prix"; "To retain the British Championship"; "To win the Monte Carlo Rally"; an event already looming up in the near future. I settled for a jocular resolution and said: "Not to puncture my rivals' tyres just before a Grand Prix."

What was the New Year to bring? In prospect, I was hopeful; in retrospect, it was patchy but not as unlucky as the year that was nearly spent. The Maserati earned its keep, but it was fickle and on several occasions let me down when I was in a winning position. No doubt I had to cane it at times to keep up with the official Italian teams, and racing cars do not like being caned, nor do racing drivers like doing it. Speed is not the prime consideration; delicate racing machinery has to be nursed and the really first-class driver is the one who can win at the slowest possible speed.

You have to take risks of a breakdown when those ahead of you set too hot a pace for effective nursing, and, obversely, the man in front needs to do no more than preserve a safe margin between himself and those chasing him. There is no point in tearing the heart out of your engine, brakes or transmission by running away from the field. Unless there is some reason. You plan your tactics as a result of practice, but you change them in accordance with the way the race is being run.

There are times, and what pleasant times they are, when you go into a race with your psychological curve, as it were, at peak. Your chances are good. Your car is as fast as any other in the race; you are absolutely fit—but you won't be if you don't train—you know the course thoroughly and there doesn't seem to be any reason why you shouldn't do well. You have to work, as do your mechanics, for this happy confidence. Practice has told you all you want to know about gear ratios, tyre pressures, etc., and your car has been prepared in accordance with your racing specifications. You have undertaken whatever is your best method of training for the event. I don't have to cut off smoking or drinking, because I don't smoke much and never drink.

Well, there we are on the starting line, a fit driver in a sound car, with the prospect of a thrilling ride ahead. If you make any mistakes, such as taking a corner too fast, it may be disastrous; but you don't "have" to, or do you? You have to concentrate all the time. Once you let your mind wander, as it is apt to do in a long-distance event, you have to bring it back with a jerk to the job in hand. More races are won on the corners than on the straights, though the importance of cornering obviously depends on the type of course, or circuit, on which you are racing. Sometimes the whole darn percentage drops to zero as, perhaps, you get brake-fade braking for a corner, and then you have to take evasive action to prevent an accident.

Then there are the races when you start with a small chance, and have to try to build it up. This has often happened to me, both on aerodrome circuits and Grand Prix courses. You know that your car is lacking in speed and power and that there are half a dozen drivers much faster than you are. You don't seem to stand much of a chance, but the race certainly isn't always to the swift. I have already explained how slip-streaming can keep you up among the faster men, but you still haven't enough power to get out of the slip-stream with your "rested engine" and sprint ahead of the man who has been towing you.

But you can adopt tactics on the corners by bluffing other drivers. You can lure a man to put on his brakes too soon or too late so that he will lose time in getting round, either by the loss of time in too soon an application or in the delay occasioned by correcting a car which has gone into the bend too fast.

Nobody in his senses would adopt any sort of "trick" which would precipitate danger, but it is perfectly legitimate to "kid" a rival into making a mistake which will cost him valuable seconds or even split seconds. In 500 c.c., colloquially known as "half-pint" racing, there is not usually a lot to choose between the speed of the cars likely to be in the vanguard, so these races are won mostly by tactics. Once, in an important race, I slip-streamed a driver for miles and so gave myself a chance to sprint off for the chequered flag, a chance to which my nursed engine responded at once to give me a narrow win.

I think the only occasion on which I have heard of deliberate misleading, to the point of introducing danger, is in the Mille Miglia. One or two competitors led the inexperienced astray by manipulating their brake lights. Quite naturally, a driver not knowing the road well would be inclined to follow the car ahead in the night hours, controlling his own car in accordance with the brake lights of the car he was tailing. Very nice, too, except when the man in front, on approaching a corner, deliberately switches off his brake lights so that when he applies the anchors there is no warning light and the poor unfortunate man behind finds himself entering the bend much too fast.

Such tactics as these are to be deplored. Not one of the top-notch drivers ever employs them. Indeed, there is a camaraderie and sportsmanship among speedmen which rules out any possibility of endangering the well-being of a rival. Baulking is completely unavoidable on some of our tracks, but it is not something which is deliberately practised.

Mind you, there is a lot of difference between the driving technique of drivers. There are those who are "killers", which means that they want to get every ounce of power out of their cars and will risk disaster rather than adopt discretion. It may be said of some of them that they are more likely to break the record for a lap than to finish a long-distance race. Their personal prowess may prevent them from crashing their cars, but they can certainly wreck them by overstressing brakes, engine and tyres. Watch racing men on the corners and you will see how some of them appear to be wrestling with their cars all the time. They are, in fact, doing just that, because they have entered the bend too fast and have to fight the steering wheel in an effort to get the car on the right line again. Actually, they appear to be faster than the man who takes his corners with the car under complete control, whereas they are usually slower and they take so much out of themselves that they are worn out, even if their car isn't, before the finish.

II

I think it is best to be as relaxed as possible when racing—physically relaxed I mean. Critics have commented on my straight-arm action because I like to sit well behind the steering wheel. Often I have had the cockpit of a car altered so as to accommodate the driving position which I find the least tiring in a long race. But you mustn't allow any mental relaxation. During such a race as Le Mans or the Mille Miglia, I have found myself thinking about such trivial things as the colour of the carpet in my London flat, or what sort of show Bud Flanagan is putting on at the Victoria Palace. But the abstraction doesn't last for long. A shake of the head and you're concentrating again. You jolly well have to. You may have marked or mentally noted braking points and corner lines, but you mustn't follow them like an automaton. As the race proceeds, brakes wear, the car gets lighter, and you have to tread on them a little sooner sometimes and later at others. Or the condition of the road surface may alter, so that you cannot stick to the drill you had formulated. What may have been safe cornering on, say, 5,500 revs., may not be safe when the track has become oily or sticky. No, when you are racing the only thing you should think about is the race itself, never forgetting to give a hasty glance at your pit personnel as you pass. They know more about the complete picture of the race than you do, and you can't win without taking directions from them.

The tensest period is during the final minutes when you are on the starting line, after the five-minute signal has been given. Somehow or other you never feel quite sure that everything is all right. I have become accustomed to it, but I have every sympathy for those drivers who put the car in and out of gear, fiddle about with things generally and are obviously in such a state of apprehensive worry that they increase their likelihood of muffing the getaway. You have to look imperturbable, even if you are not. It is always a great relief when you feel your tyres biting into the surface and feel the surge of acceleration as you race away. Not that you always do; oh dear no. Just a little bit of over-revving and you may find your wheels spinning away while the other competitors sprint away from you. I prefer the Le Mans type of running start where you have to dash across the road and start up your engine. It's great fun, especially if you can get a bit of advantage, and practice helps this.

Always the Monte Carlo rally opens up the year's competitions and nearly always it causes something of a stir, either by reason of the freakish conditions or because somebody or other objects to the method of scoring marks. This year (1954) was no exception. Once again I drove in the official Sunbeam team with Des Scannell and John Cooper as co-drivers, and we started from Athens.

We had a fairly easy time of it. There were bits of snow and ice here and there, but conditions generally were fair. The number of competitors who finished on time at Monte Carlo must have constituted a record, and so the result depended on the eliminating tests, one of which was a speed and regularity trial over the last 165 miles of the rally route and then a "round-the-houses" race in Monte Carlo. In the former, the idea was to get over the Col de Leques as fast as possible and then to average the same speed over three other sections, varying in length. We were fastest on the Col, but the famous Louis Chiron, a native of Monte Carlo, had us beaten all ends up on the regularity part of the business. Local knowledge counted for a good deal, and Chiron was a good enough driver to capitalise on his knowledge.

Sunbeams scored their second consecutive team victory

and Louis Chiron won the rally. But there was no prize-giving as is usual. An objection was lodged against Chiron's car, a Lancia, on the grounds that it did not conform to the regulations, and then there was the question as to whether another team had beaten the Sunbeams, which wasn't the fact, because, as is right and proper, teams have to be nominated before the start of the rally and the other team had not been so nominated. Anyway, the awards were withheld and it was not until some weeks afterwards that Chiron's victory was confirmed.

There was a quaint affair near the ancient town of Sestrières, in the Alpine country. It seems that some enterprising youths, with an ingenious idea for making some francs for themselves, had traced a number of wheel tracks on the snow-covered road leading them into a field where the snow was at such a depth that as the competitors followed the tracks they found themselves well and truly embedded. As they struggled to extricate themselves, along came the perpetrators of the hoax, demanding money for assistance in getting them back on the road. There was a police inquiry into the matter, but as far as I know the miscreants got away with it.

I gather there was a similar incident in Germany during the rally some years ago, when some British competitors were decoyed into an immense snowdrift which was probably more artificial than real. Standing by the drift was a powerful lorry with towing-chain all ready, but the number of marks they asked for towing the car out of the drift was immense. One of the party smelt a rat and after a lot of haggling, agreed to pay the sum demanded. So the tow was accomplished, and the car came out of the drift like a cork from a bottle. A suspicious member of the crew nonchalantly detached the towing-chain while another member ostentatiously withdrew his note-case as though to pay. At a signal, the team jumped into the car, whose engine had already been started, and away they went, leaving the "highwaymen" shouting and gesticulating behind them.

114

III

My next engagement was in the Sebring race in Florida, for which a first-class entry representative of Europe's strength in motor racing had been engaged, but before I left, there were certain social engagements to be fulfilled. I was getting more than my share of invitations to appear on quizzes, to judge various things from feminine beauty to newspaper competitions and to be a sort of Exhibit "A" with other sporting celebrities.

On one occasion I got a bit of a shock owing to my absent-mindedness. My case containing passport, travellers' cheques and other documents disappeared a few days before I was due to leave for Florida. I thought they'd been taken out of my car, and if you think the contents of a car are safe just because the doors are locked, you can think again. This time, however, it was nothing of the sort. I had left the case in a bookshop, and within a few hours it was returned.

Off then to the United States, where everybody is most hospitable but just don't know how to make tea, which was then one of my favourite beverages. In Florida, they have a quaint idea of putting a minute dose of tea into a little muslin bag and dangling it in the pot. They don't seem to know that to brew tea properly the water must be boiling.

I had been offered an Italian Osca for the big race at Sebring by the American enthusiast Briggs Cunningham, an American who had shown a lively interest in European racing and particularly Le Mans. This was a most generous offer because all Briggs could get was a few hundred more hard racing miles added to his car and possibly worse. I had asked Jags. for a car but was turned down; however, they released me to drive the baby O.S.C.A. with Bill Lloyd, Briggs' nephew. I can honestly say that these two people plus a really fine little car made this one of my most enjoyable races, and certainly my most unexpected! The English party included Reg Parnell, Roy Salvadori, Peter Collins and Pat Griffiths, who were teamed up for an Aston Martin challenge. Leaving at about the same time was a strong Continental contingent including Juan Fangio and Alberto Ascari who, not surprisingly, were the two favourites for the big event. Lancias were making a determined bid for racing honours in the U.S.A., for joining Fangio and Ascari were Piero Taruffi and Villoresi.

It was not a Grand Prix event, but was included in the series in which points were awarded for the World's Sports Car Championship. Sebring is an aerodrome cum road track with quite a few bends, and has an extremely English atmosphere about it, the bends being named Castrol Corner, KLG Curve, Austin Bend, Dunlop Turn, etc.

During practice the well-manned Lancia cars simply wiped up the field on speed, and at the start of the race their victory seemed as near a racing certainty as possible. They had plenty of speed, but in a twelve-hours' endurance race fast motoring isn't everything. Our Osca—built by the Maserati Brothers—was completely outpowered and outspeeded by the Italian team, and so were practically all the other cars in the race.

There were 58 starters, and after two hours there were the Lancia boys, Ascari, Fangio and Taruffi miles away from anybody. We were lapped time after time. Neither of us had ideas any more ambitious than to finish, in the hope of winning the handicap prize. But it was a real ten little nigger boys case, with the fastest of the cars dropping out one by one. First Ascari was out with back-axle trouble and then Fangio found his gear-box out of commission, but still Taruffi was way out in the lead.

After eight hours, as a result of the process of elimination, we were lying second to Taruffi, but way behind and were having trouble with our brakes. Then came disaster to Lancia hopes. Taruffi stalled two miles from the pits and began to

116

push in an attempt to save the situation. It so exhausted him that they had to carry him off the track. His co-driver Manzon jumped into the car and tried to get it going. No good—a broken valve had finished it.

We knew nothing about this at the time, but we did know that with Taruffi out we were actually in the lead, with the sole remaining Lancia about a couple of laps behind. By this time the brakes had just ceased to function, and the only way to round the corners was to broadside the car. But we lasted to the finish and won, on one of the smallest cars in the race; it was a complete triumph for reliability as distinct from speed. That was what the racecourse fellows call a clean-up for the book. Nobody, least of all Bill Lloyd or myself, had expected us to win in such a field.

If ever an event proved that a race is not over until the chequered flag falls, that was it. With only just over an hour to go we were many miles behind the lead with inoperative brakes. Curious that the great champions should all have crumpled up while, in a similar way, the little-known Valenzano and Rubirosa (incidentally, he was the Dominican diplomat known as "the playboy") should have finished second. The best performance in a British car was that of the Austin Healey driven by Lance Macklin and the American, George Huntoon, who finished third.

Thus 1954 had started well for me, with a share of a team victory in the Monte Carlo and then this dramatic and very surprising win in the first of the big international races.

Was it an augury of a successful year? No, it wasn't, at least not for a time. Clutch trouble at Goodwood; then retirement in the British Empire Trophy race at Oulton Park, the new Cheshire track, with clutch trouble again. I like Oulton. It has many natural hazards, is undulating and a change from the aerodromes. As a professional driver, I naturally welcomed any addition to the number of race tracks, but here was something really different, simulating road conditions more than any of the other circuits.

Check to the barren period came at Silverstone in May, where I won the 500 c.c. race. Not so good in the International Trophy race, which was the big event of the meeting, for while lying second on my Maserati, the de Dion tube broke. I had to be content with third on a Jaguar in the Production Touring Car race, but the bad luck streak had been broken. A few days later I took the Cooper Norton to the Nurburgring and collected another first—still among the half-pinters, you'll notice.

There had recently been completed at what was purported to be a cost of something like £100,000, a new circuit alongside the famous Grand National course at Aintree, Liverpool. In May, the first international meeting was held there with the *Daily Telegraph* sponsoring it and the British Automobile Racing Club running it. The circuit, beautifully surfaced, was what might be called a driver's course in that it called for really expert manipulation of the cars on the rather tight bends. I entered my Cooper Norton for the 500 c.c. event and the Maserati for the Formula Libre International race.

Although I had driven the Maserati at Bordeaux and Silverstone without scoring with it, I had got its "feel" and it handled extremely well. Opposition in the big event included the powerful Thinwall Special, with young Peter Collins at the wheel; a couple of B.R.M.s, driven by Ken Wharton and Ron Flockhart; Reg Parnell on a Ferrari; Roy Salvadori on a Maserati and Jean Behra on a Gordini.

I was in first-class company, but not in first-class condition owing to a shocking cold, which wasn't helped by the wet dismal weather. The crowd was disappointing; no doubt the vile conditions kept people away, though the covered accommodation was better than at any other British circuit, because the normal Grand National stands did duty for motor racing. I qualified for the final by running into third place in my heat behind Reg Parnell and Peter Collins, and before the final came on I had run away with the 500 c.c. race.

Overhead conditions were better when the 19 finalists lined up for the Trophy race over a distance of 100 miles. As at Sebring, I hadn't the speed of several of the other competitors and when we slid off on the wet track Collins took the Thinwall to the head of affairs, followed by the snarling B.R.M.s in the hands of Wharton and Flockhart, and then by Reg Parnell, with me in fifth place. Collins was able to increase his lead on every lap, and while chasing him in second place Flockhart ran out of road on the fifth lap and lost a lap. Parnell's Ferrari was not going too well, and I was able to pass him for third place with Jean Behra making every effort to drive me out of it. Then I shot past Wharton and was second, but what seemed like an enormously long 40 seconds behind Peter.

By the half distance, I had knocked this down to 20 seconds; then the Thinwall blew up and went into the retiring bay and I was in front with Parnell and Flockhart, who had made a fine recovery after his skid, chasing me home. Wharton's B.R.M. had fallen back with brake trouble. I was not caught, however, and, indeed, increased my lead. It was a nice, comfortable ride. I had won because of the misfortune that had attended faster runners, so I couldn't complain about gremlins, especially after my lucky win at Sebring. The Maserati had gained its first success and had definitely started paying for its keep.

What a remarkable manifestation of what might be termed numerological superstition. I always try to get No. 7 in every race, and it was with this number painted on my car that I won luckily at Aintree at an average speed of 77·7 m.p.h.! Must be something in this mystic seven business.

10

THE GERMANS COME BACK

I

THERE was excitement when it was announced by Mr. W. Lyons that a new type of Jaguar had been built and would make a strong challenge for the Le Mans 24-Hour race. The new Jaguars looked magnificent, beautifully streamlined and low built. With the thoroughness which is the handmaiden of success on the race tracks, a prototype was taken over to Le Mans; the circuit was closed and a trial run was made; 115 miles an hour was clocked on one practice lap, which was 3 miles an hour faster than the best achieved by last year's winners, Tony Rolt and Duncan Hamilton. Prospects then were excellent, and I was delighted to be offered the wheel of one of the three entered for Le Mans, with Peter Walker as co-driver.

Well, the Jaguar bid failed, but my goodness, what a race it was! Gonzales on a big Ferrari set the pace from the start, and it soon became obvious that it was to be a duel between the Italian cars and the British Jaguars. But with the race about half over, two Jaguars and two Ferraris were out of it. I had all the excitement I wanted. At round about the seventh hour, travelling down the Mulsanne Straight at about 150 miles an hour, I braked for a corner, but got little response. Thank goodness there is an escape road there, and using the gear-box to pull down the speed, I drove the car up it. Most unpleasant when you tread on the brakes and find there aren't any!

Gonzales and Duncan Hamilton made a terrific fight of

it, and produced one of the most exciting finishes ever seen on the Le Mans circuit. Towards the closing stages Gonzales, with a lead of over ten minutes, pulled into the pits and stayed there for six or seven minutes. Then his car refused to start for a while. When he finally got away Hamilton, also in the pits, was 3½ minutes behind. The rain-swept circuit was sodden but Hamilton, who is a very daring driver, began to overhaul the leader. He picked up valuable seconds on every lap, and with half an hour to go had reduced Gonzales' lead to less than two minutes. At the finish, Gonzales crossed the line 105 seconds ahead, which isn't much of a margin in a 24 hours' race. Disappointing to the Jaguar camp, but nevertheless an excellent performance with their 3½-litre cars ranged against the 5-litre Ferraris.

As usual, Le Mans was followed by the Belgian Grand Prix on the Spa circuit, and there we all were again, ready to do battle on one of the fastest circuits in Europe. I drove my own Maserati, but I was no match for the works cars and Fangio didn't have much trouble in holding off the rest of the field, though Maurice Trintignant finished a close second. I managed to win third place, again owing to the failure of faster cars, so that my Maserati was at least proving its reliability even if it wasn't quite fast enough for the official works cars driven by the leading exponents of the game. It was here that the factory introduced a new head for the engine giving 30 b.h.p. more.

Poor Mike Hawthorn had a trying ordeal. He was racing extremely well and was up among the leaders when an escape from an exhaust system threatened to asphyxiate him. With difficulty, he managed to pull up his car as poisonous fumes surged up from the cockpit. He drove it to the pits where Gonzales took over, but found he had had enough of it after a single lap.

Fangio averaged just over 115 m.p.h. for the entire race, and he could have been even faster had he been more closely pressed.

121

The French Grand Prix meeting at Rheims offered Jaguars a chance of revenging themselves on Ferrari after the Le Mans race, for the Grand Prix itself was preceded by a twelve hours' race in which both marques were engaged, the three Jaguars being manned by the same teams that raced at Le Mans. I was given the job of pacemaker and wrecker, and set a pace from the start, with a first lap at over 110 miles an hour, in the dark.

The three Jaguars were lying first, third and fourth for a time, with only the American, Briggs Cunningham, splitting them. We kept the lead for nearly five hours at over 115 miles an hour before transmission trouble put us out of the race, after which Ken Wharton and Peter Whitehead were able to take command. They stayed in front to the finish with Tony Rolt and Duncan Hamilton in second place, ready to move up if and when necessary.

Jean Behra put himself out by ramming one of the Jaguars and smashing the front of his Gordini without seriously impeding the Jaguar. Wharton and Whitehead made no mistake, however, and ran out winners at an average speed of just over 104 miles an hour, with Rolt and Hamilton second and a Belgian pair, Laurent and Swaters, in third place for Jaguars. The Rheims twelve-hour race does not compare in importance with Le Mans, but Jaguars had certainly taken partial revenge with a 1–2–3 victory.

II

The next day was to be one of the most significant in all the post-war years of motor racing for, for the first time, Mercedes were back in the fold, with Juan Fangio leading a German team in the French Grand Prix. His team mates were Karl Kling and Hans Hermann, two well-known drivers but not quite of the power and speed of the great Fangio. It will be recalled that the Germans, with the Mercedes and Auto Unions, had carried all before them in the classic races of the pre-war era, and their come-back was successful and dramatic. Fangio led practically all the way on his white car; Hans Hermann set up a lap record at 121·45 m.p.h., and Karl Kling finished second behind the maestro. Ferraris, Maseratis and Gordinis were all whacked by the Germans; Fangio won at the terrific average of over 115 m.p.h. Mike Hawthorn was again unlucky. The engine of his Ferrari blew up, and left him no option but to save himself by taking an escape road.

Those new Mercedes were very impressive indeed, and there was a great deal of speculation about their chances in the year's classic events. It was generally expected that they would give battle to France and Italy in the G.P. contests and would also menace the supremacy of the British in sports car racing. It was a threat which was not only to materialise, but which was to be eminently successful. Certainly the writing was on the wall at Rheims, and it was written in German characters.

The Germans had decided to enter for the British Grand Prix at Silverstone in the following month, and with a fine entry from Italy, there were all the makings of a grand international contest. Their showing was sufficiently impressive at Rheims to give evidence that they would swoop down on Silverstone and take the Grand Prix back home with them. It didn't turn out that way. Indeed, the German showing at Silverstone produced more ignominy than glory.

Before going to Silverstone, however, there was the Alpine Trial to compete in and owing to the abnormal weather conditions it proved to be one of the most difficult of the series. I drove a Sunbeam, and by completing the course without loss of marks, not only won an Alpine Cup, but also became the second winner—the first was Ian Appleyard —to win a Gold Cup, signifying the rather difficult "hat-trick" of winning a cup three years running.

It was a wet day for Silverstone, but such was the magnet-like attraction of the German Mercedes that a terrific crowd, estimated at 90,000, went to see them try to confirm their great victory at Rheims. Only Juan Fangio and Karl Kling represented Germany, and they were opposed by a half-dozen Ferraris and a like number of Maseratis. The Mercedes were of rather unusual design. They were equipped with five-speed gear-boxes and fuel injection, but also had enveloping bodies which I feel were difficult to handle because poor Fangio kept hitting the marker barrels. In practice, Fangio had beaten 100 m.p.h. for a lap, but on the wet track neither his nor Kling's Mercedes had the stability of the Ferraris or the Maseratis.

At the drop of the flag it was Gonzales who sped away to the lead, with Fangio close up and then Mike Hawthorn on a Ferrari, with my Maserati in fourth place, keeping them all in sight. For lap after lap it was a real dog fight, with Gonzales still in front and Hawthorn and myself holding Fangio. Then came a big German blow. Kling spun off the track on the second Mercedes, and lost time. Fangio wasn't happy. Driving behind him, it was possible to see that he was having a lot of difficulty with his car on the greasy track. My Maserati was going well, and in a little while passed both Hawthorn and Fangio and took second place. Fine while it lasted, but it didn't last long enough, for with ten laps to go, transmission trouble stopped me and I could only crawl into the pits with Gonzales and Hawthorn fighting it out.

"Faster" signs were hung out from the German pits, but neither Kling nor Fangio could respond, and eventually Gonzales and Hawthorn brought home the Ferraris in first and second places. Marimon brought his Maserati into third place, and poor Fangio could do no better than fourth. What a mighty ovation Mike got for finishing second behind Gonzales; even greater, it seemed, than the cheers for the winner.

But there was dismay in the German pits. It turned out to be the last mistake of the camp, for they modified their cars and went on to score consistently in most of the classics that were to follow. It sounds almost like monotonous re-iteration, but again I won a consolation prize by leading the field in the 500 c.c. race.

III

I had a wonderful scrap at Caen in the International race with Maurice Trintignant shortly after Silverstone, in pouring rain. After leading him for 16 of the 60 laps, he passed me in great style. I hung on and then, with about 8 laps to go, took my Maserati past his Ferrari, but Maurice came past again and I just couldn't catch him. I finished three seconds behind, but it wasn't a bad performance in a privately owned car against a works-prepared car.

Then came the German Grand Prix, which this year was also the European Grand Prix, on the famous Nurburgring. Mercedes who, after the Silverstone débâcle, had scuttled back home to diagnose the troubles which had beset them, had to do something about it. It would have been terrible to them if, in front of their own people, they were to get beaten by the Italians. But there was no panic. They modified the bodies; they improved the steering and were soon able to show, in practice, that they were a match for anybody. It was here that I was asked to share the No. 1 position at Maseratis with poor Marimon, who was killed during practice.

When the flag dropped Fangio, with his very low bottom gear, screamed away from us and went to the front, but he was soon passed by Gonzales who, to the enormous crowd's dismay, was the first to complete a lap. Fangio was on his tail, followed by myself, Lang and Hermann in the other Mercedes. Second, third and fourth was very nice team work, but it wasn't what the crowd wanted, which was Fangio at the head of the field. They did not have to wait long, for the great Argentinian got into his stride in the second lap and passed Gonzales. I was soon out with a broken con-rod.

Mike Hawthorn did not last much longer. Later in the race he took over Gonzales' car in a hopeless attempt to catch Fangio. There was something of a sensation when Kling overtook Fangio and started some real dicing, but that didn't worry the maestro, who drove almost throughout on a tight rein because there was nobody who could really challenge him. He finally won comfortably at 82·77 m.p.h., which wasn't very fast, but bore out the theory that the best way to win a race is at the slowest possible speed at which you can keep your competitors at bay. The Hawthorn-Gonzales Ferrari was second and Trintignant headed off Kling for third place in another Ferrari. Battle honours to Mercedes.

There was a touch of the old Neubauer when Kling came in for adjustments near the finish. A great crowd swarmed round the pit to watch proceedings, but the greatest of all pit managers wasn't going to have any sort of interference with his pit men's duties. With a roar like an angry bull he frightened the crowd away, leaving a clear space for the work to be done, while a great roar of delight and approval came from the stands. It is possible that he remonstrated with Kling for going "haywire" and taking risks when it was his job to play for safety, for as a result of his very daring driving after overtaking Fangio, he apparently did a little overstressing and deranged the suspension.

After the German Grand Prix I flew back for a big meeting at Brands Hatch. What a contrast that little "kidney"-shaped circuit provided to the winding, mountainous Nurburgring. There was a big crowd estimated at 40,000 there to see the sport. The big event was the International Challenge Trophy for Formula 3 (500 c.c.) cars, run in three 7-lap heats and a 10-lap final. I had to start in the back row in my heat because I had not been able to put in any practice laps—you can't very well when you're flying back from Germany. But it was easy enough to qualify for the final.

We had quite a scrap in this, with Lewis Evans, Ivor

Bueb and myself engaged in a real dog fight until I was able to shake them off and go after the leader, Jim Russell, a first-class exponent of the art of driving "tiddlers". Try as I would, I could not get by and he held premier position throughout. So he won a very deserved victory.

My turn was to come, for within a week we were at Oulton Park, with the Maserati and a Cooper. I like Oulton Park and apparently it likes me, for I really came home this time. Chief event was for a Gold Cup over 36 laps—100 miles. Once again I was relegated to the back row because of no practising on the Maserati, which had been put into good order after throwing a con-rod in Germany. She was running beautifully, and soon overtook the field, led by Reg Parnell on a Ferrari.

I was able to establish quite a commanding lead, and the Maserati was running well, so that in the later stages of the race I was able to beat the record for the course. Roy Salvadori, driving his usual race with daring and control, had a very narrow squeak. He was trying to get on terms with Reg Parnell in second place when, on rounding one of the bends, his brakes failed. He went full-tilt into a sizable tree but jumped clear. His car was reduced to a wreck.

There was another race for Formula 1 cars, this time over 20 laps (55 miles). I had the fastest car, and having quickly got the lead found myself unchallenged, so that I won at 82·91 miles an hour, which was a shade under the average of 83·48 miles registered in the big race. Just to round off a very nice day I won the 75-mile race for Formula 3 cars, also easily, and who was the man who followed me home in second place? None other than Jim Russell, the man who had beaten me at Brands Hatch a few days earlier.

IV

Next stop Switzerland—I shall have to think about seeing what can be done about a season ticket for flying between home and the Continent. Here, the world's finest drivers were ranged against each other in full strength, with a terrific fight over the 300 miles distance in prospect between the Mercedes, Ferraris and the Maseratis. In the second day's practice, despite torrential rain, I went round the Bremgarten circuit in 2 minutes 56 seconds, nine seconds faster than Gonzales on the No. 1 Ferrari and 2·7 seconds faster than Fangio on the Mercedes. Consternation in the rival camps —I was driving officially for Maserati—and a little incredulity at my own pit. To show that there had been no mistake I went out again and equalled the time, which served to startle the opposition further.

Fifteen cars waited for the flag to start on a day which, as a change from the dreadful weather we had been having, broke fine. Only eight finished, and I wasn't one of them. Why the dickens does that gremlin start crawling around in all the classic races? Perhaps the fine weather reduced my chances, because the Maserati was apparently easier to handle in wet conditions than the faster Mercedes.

I got off to a good start, but had not the acceleration of Fangio, who made his customary spring for leadership, followed by Gonzales (Ferrari) and Karl Kling (Mercedes). I passed Kling on the first lap—a very fast one—for third place and so the picture was already beginning to develop into an exciting triangle: Mercedes, Ferrari, Maserati.

Fangio stayed where he was, but soon he had lost his team mate, Karl Kling, who spun at a corner, crashed into the straw bales and dented the back of his car. There was great joy in the Maserati pits a little later when I was able to get by Gonzales in the Ferrari; I was now second to Fangio, but a devil of a long way behind him. We stayed like that for lap after lap, with Gonzales and Mike Hawthorn chasing us quite close enough to keep the speed verging on the 100 m.p.h. Then my horses began to falter. First Hawthorn, then Gonzales passed me, and gradually I slowed down until the engine packed up altogether in the 22nd lap. Then

(Above): Stirling Moss driving a 1956 Works Grand Prix Maserati, a car with which he had many successes. Note that although he is wearing a vizor on his crash helmet a pair of goggles is worn round his neck. *(Photo: T. C. March)*

(Below): With the Type 250F Grand Prix Maserati at Aintree. With this car Stirling had a spectacular run of successes on the Aintree Circuit. *(Photo: Autocar)*

(*Above*): Whilst mechanics work on the engine of the transporter van, Alf Francis and Tony Robson, Stirling's two mechanics, prepare the Type 250F Grand Prix Maserati. During the course of a normal season this combination of mechanics, transporter and racing car travel many thousands of miles, and the mechanics virtually "live" in the transporter. (*Photo by courtesy of Rootes*)

(*Below*): Silverstone 1956 with the 3-litre works Maserati sports car. This car in many ways was similar to, and its design was influenced by the Type 250F Grand Prix Maserati. (*Photo by courtesy of BP*)

Mike ran into trouble and had to retire, so that the race became no more than a duel between the two compatriots, Juan Fangio and Frolian Gonzales.

It wasn't a match. Fangio had much greater speed, and just kept in front from the start to the finish, to win another Mercedes victory at an average speed for the 300 miles of over 99 miles an hour, which, even on so fast a course as Bremgarten, is going some. By his victory, Fangio had put himself in an unassailable position for the World's Championship, and there never was a man on whom the title sat so becomingly.

The Championship is awarded on a points basis in the nine classic races of the year, the Grand Prix events of Belgium, France, Great Britain, Germany, Switzerland, Italy and Spain, the Indianapolis 500 miles race and the Argentine Grand Prix. Eight points are awarded for a win, six for second, four for third, three for fourth and two for fifth. The Grand Prix regulations permit for changing of drivers, and in that case the points are divided between them. Fangio, before winning the Swiss Grand Prix, had won the Argentine, Belgian, French and German classics, and so was out of everybody's reach. Incidentally, it should be mentioned that an extra point is awarded for the fastest lap in any of the classic races and that if there is a tie, then it is the first to have achieved it who scores.

The Grand Prix of Pescara, not one of the events on the Championship calendar, but still an important race, was very largely a domestic affair between the Maserati and Ferrari stables, with none of the impressive silver Mercedes engaged. The circuit is a rather difficult one of just under 16 miles, and it had to be covered sixteen times. My Maserati, which had been extremely well tuned by the works, seemed to have a fair chance of winning. I had done the fastest practice lap; I went away at the start and with nobody sitting on my tail held the lead for three laps, then, high up in the mountains, the engine failed, leaving me absolutely fed up with the long run of misfortune which had attended my efforts in Grand Prix races.

Prince Birabongse, generally known as Bira, took on the leadership, but was delayed when he dropped an exhaust-pipe and eventually finished second to L. Musso. All the Ferraris fell out, leaving Maseratis to take the first four places, with Jean Behra and C. Bucchi following them on Gordinis. Only three competitors, Musso, Bira and the Franco-American, Harry Schell, actually completed the full distance.

Even more disappointing to me was the Italian Grand Prix at Monza. All the drivers who had any real chance of winning had, of course, a good knowledge of the Monza circuit which was just under 4 miles a lap. Fangio was there with the Mercedes, but in spite of his victory at Berne he was by no means regarded as invincible, because Mercedes had not shown any really pronounced superiority, although they had done so well. Ferrari and Maserati were both prepared to take on the Germans on their own beloved Monza.

Everybody was anxious to get a good position on the starting line, and practising was fast and furious. Finally, Fangio, Ascari and myself were split by a mere fraction of a second in practice times, and took front row on the grid.

German acceleration again made its mark, and at the end of the first lap Karl Kling was a length or so ahead of Fangio in 2 minutes 1 second—a mere 116·37 m.p.h. But Kling paid the penalty of his spectacular driving. He spun round on to the grass verge and fell behind. Gonzales slip-streamed Fangio for a few laps, and then went in front, but the brilliant Ascari now took a turn and whipped his car out of the close formation leaders and headed them all. I was quite happy to lie third or fourth during these preliminary tactics. The speed remained high—round about 111 m.p.h., and there wasn't much of a chance of it dropping off, because Ascari and Fangio were having a real scrap at the head of affairs, passing and repassing each other.

I was still "sitting pretty" when, just before the half distance, Villoresi shot past to sneak third position, Ascari having taken the lead from Fangio, though he could hold on to it by only a few yards. Two laps later, Villoresi blew up, and with Fangio in some sort of trouble so that he was occasionally hitting the grass verge, I was able to pass him and set off in pursuit of Ascari. I am told that for the next half-hour or so the spectators were treated to one of the biggest thrills Grand Prix racing had produced. I stormed by Ascari, but he wasn't standing for that. He went by me and then we raced almost bonnet to bonnet until the pace, now over 112 m.p.h., deranged Ascari's engine. So instead of having a most exciting duel with Ascari I was, for a little while, on my own in front. I think it was the first time I had ever occupied the lead in a Grande Epreuve.

Soon the silver Mercedes of Fangio began to edge up to me; it passed me, but not greatly to my concern, for it sounded woolly and, in fact, began to drop back. Was I, at last, going to win one of the really big races? It really seemed so; the car was behaving extremely well and I was increasing my lead on practically every lap. Higher and higher went the average speed; I could not afford to slacken up at all, not with men like Fangio, Mike Hawthorn and Gonzales chasing me. With twelve laps to go and sixty-eight behind me, I had the really commanding advantage of 20 seconds, and there was not the slightest sign of the engine packing up under the strain. Then disaster overtook me. The oil tank split and the poor old engine was starved of lubricant. I stopped at the pits to take aboard more oil, but the damage was done.

I limped along for a couple of laps or so, and then pushed the car very nearly a mile so that I could lurk by the finishing line and push over to become an official finisher. Fangio went on to win narrowly from Mike Hawthorn and Gonzales at just under 112 m.p.h., I might fairly say that I came very near to winning my first Grand Prix race on the Continent.

Hard luck in a way; but after all, Grand Prix races have to be held over a minimum distance and are intended to be a test of endurance as well as speed. To regard the matter logically, the fact is that the Maserati just did not stand up to the full distance.

It was a fine race while it lasted, especially when we were all jockeying for the lead or the retention of our positions, in the first half of the race. The Italian spectators, who are always more ostentatious in their praise than a British crowd, went wild with excitement and I must say that they cheered me as loudly and as enthusiastically as they did their own beloved Ascari and Villoresi. Stairling Moose, as they called me, had had a go.

Over to Ireland for the Tourist Trophy Race, in which I was to drive a Jaguar. It was a gloomy day at Dundrod; the car was not running up to standard, eventually got tired and broke down, and I found myself doing my old trick of waiting on the finishing line so that, after the chequered flag had dropped, I could push over the line to occupy the lowly place of eighteenth, but nevertheless as an official finisher.

The race was decided on handicap, and went to the little D.B. Panhard driven by Paul Armagnac and Gerard Loreau, but the real hero of the race was Mike Hawthorn, who drove his Ferrari magnificently, with Trintignant as co-driver to ward off the challenge of the great Ascari and Fangio in Lancias and win the award for the car putting up the fastest average time. Their most excellent performance ensured for Ferraris the Sports Car Championship of the World for 1954.

The Goodwood International Meeting wound up the English programme for the year, except for a meeting at Aintree, and it produced some fine racing and excellent results for me. The chief event was the Goodwood Trophy, a fifty-mile race for Grand Prix type cars. Opposition to my Maserati came from Peter Collins on the Vanwall Special; Roy Salvadori (Maserati); Reg Parnell (Ferrari) and half a dozen other drivers.

Parnell dashed away in front, but blew up and left me the leadership, which I was able to retain in spite of the efforts of Peter Collins to bring the Vanwall along. More exciting, if not so productive, was the Formula Libre event for the Woodcote Cup. Peter Collins had the Thinwall Special, Ken Wharton a B.R.M., myself the Maserati, and Mike Hawthorn the Vanwall Special. Peter couldn't be touched. He went away with the lead in the second lap and held it for all ten laps, with the B.R.M. screaming behind it.

But what a wonderful dust-up I had with Mike! With his disc brakes he seemed able to catch me on braking, but I left him at other places and throughout the race we were duelling almost at each other's elbows. I managed to get over the line about half a length ahead in third place. A second in the sports car race and another in a 500 c.c. event, which was nearly a photographic finish with Don Parker, completed quite a busy but successful day's racing.

Aintree, with an International Meeting sponsored by the *Daily Telegraph*, proved to be even better than the Goodwood International. There was a big crowd to see the mixed grill of racing, and it was gratifying to win the curtain-raiser for 500 c.c.s at 77·53 m.p.h., but the event that really mattered was the Formula 1 race over 17 laps for the *Daily Telegraph* Trophy. I had a works Maserati, as also did Mantovani. Mike Hawthorn drove the Vanwall, on which Mr. Tony Vandervell was spending a lot of money in order to base a Grand Prix team, and Jean Behra (Gordini), Louis Rosier (Maserati) and Reg Parnell (Ferrari) established quite an imposing list of those on the starting grid.

The flag went down, and I went off with a clear track ahead of me and the others following in close formation. The first lap showed me that I was more or less in command, provided that everything went smoothly, so I just carried on, increased my lead without unduly pressing and, with Mike dropping back, was in an almost unassailable position at the half distance. Hawthorn improved later and passed Harry Schell to win second place in the last lap.

To finish off the day's racing there was a Formula Libre race over 17 laps. I was again driving the Maserati, but in a rather different field because the Thinwall Special, reputedly the fastest car in the country, and the B.R.M. were eligible. There were two B.R.M.s with Ken Wharton and Ron Flockhart at the wheels, but they did not come into the picture, for Ken quickly retired with a broken oil-pipe and Flockhart could not keep up with the leaders. Peter Collins went into the lead at once with the Thinwall Special, and after dogging him for a bit I passed in the sixth lap. Mike Hawthorn had already dropped out with the Vanwall, and soon the Thinwall went out as well, so that the rest of the race was an easy thing for me and I went over the line well ahead of Mantovani, with Flockhart bringing the B.R.M. into third place. That meant I had achieved the hat-trick, which was a very satisfying round-off for the 1954 season at home.

11

I JOIN MERCEDES

I

I COULD look back on the year with some satisfaction, but not very jubilantly. I had done well in the Formula 3 division and had been moderately successful with the Maserati. December was a wonderful month for me. It brought me the award of my fourth Gold Star, and, a little later, a trophy in which I take very great pride. Each year the Guild of Motoring Writers nominates the man whom it considers to be the driver of the year. Nominations are sent in from members of the Guild in various countries and the final vote is taken at the French Motor Show. This year, the Guild awarded their "Oscar" to me and it was duly presented at the annual dinner of the Guild in December.

Then, too, I was placed fifth in the list of the year's leading British Sportsmen by the Sports Writers' Association, and I was in first-class company. The leading six were: (1) Dr. Roger Bannister (remember that wonderful "under four" mile he had done); (2) Chris Chataway (with his world's running record for 5,000 metres); (3) Don Cockell (British and Empire Heavyweight Boxing Champion); (4) Cyril Peacock (World's Amateur Sprint Cycling Championship); (5) Stirling Moss and (6) Geoffrey Duke (World's Senior Motor-cycle Race Champion).

Honours in plenty for my achievements during the year, but before the curtain fell on 1954 I was to receive the sensational and most encouraging news that the German Mercedes firm was ready and anxious to sign me as one of their official Grand Prix team for 1955. It is not easy, now, properly to analyse my feelings when the news reached me in America. I had gone over there to compete in what was called the "Mountain Rally", and had driven a Sunbeam in a trio of cars which won the team prize. When I heard the news of the Mercedes offer, I was a little awed, a little bewildered, and very pleased. With all my experience, I had not done a lot of real racing in the Grand Prix series on cars which stood a real chance. True, I had led the Maserati team for the latter half of the year, but to have a place in that all-conquering team—and I felt in my bones that it would be all-conquering—was to give me an unique personal opportunity.

They tell me that I am inclined to be restless; certainly I could think of nothing but to get back to England and consolidate the Mercedes offer. Until it came I had more or less decided to re-sign for Maseratis, but had not done so because of the whisperings and talk of a Mercedes offer. Many people thought I had signed. The Italian firm protested most positively that they had my signature, but since the agreement still lay unsigned on my desk, they were obviously under some misapprehension.

The way was clear for me to negotiate with Mercedes, I flew back across the Atlantic as soon as I could, and, changing planes at London Airport, flew to meet the German executives and try out the car. All the motor magazines and a lot of the national and provincial papers were discussing the subject of "Moss and Mercedes". There were many reports based on the supposition that I had already signed for Maserati; there were comments on the policy of driving a foreign car; there were all sorts of stories about the value of the contract offered, the generally estimated amount being £25,000. Of course this was absolutely ridiculous.

On the whole, the Press was generous. They accepted my statement, which was entirely sincere, that my ultimate ambition was to win the World Championship in a British car, but that there was very little hope of doing so during the following year, and that as a professional racer I really had no option but to accept the offer.

Arriving in Germany, I found all prepared for testing. We went to the very fast Hockenheim motor-cycle racing circuit. The track was wet but there, awaiting me, were the 3-litre sports car and the superb 2½-litre Formula 1 Grand Prix model. I did a few laps, "feeling my way" as it were, and then gave the G.P. model the gun. At once I knew, in spite of its strangeness, that here was a car which gave me everything I could desire.

I fumbled the five-speed gear-box until I got used to it. The reason for this was the gate change was back to front to what was usual. I tied with Karl Kling's record; I maintained the speed and appeared to impress the experts who were watching me drive against the clock. They said afterwards that they had intended to sign me on, however I performed on that demonstration; but there was my side of the bargain to consider as well. I had no intention of blindly signing on the dotted line before having had a chance of trying out the cars.

Anyway, everybody appeared to be satisfied, and so the die was cast. I was to drive Mercedes in all the classic "Grande Epreuve" races next year, but apart from other specified engagements with the sports model, I was free to accept engagements so long as they did not interfere with the German programme, in which I must be "first claim". Nothing could have suited me better. It was no longer to be a matter of scratching around on unsuitable cars; I should take part in all the events counting for the World Championship, with the backing of a very sound and thorough organisation behind me.

I was not to be the leader of the team. No. 1 position was rightly filled by the World Champion, Juan Fangio, but never again should I be able to complain that

I had not had the opportunity of gaining Grand Prix experience. I might not be able to win the world title just yet, but I ought to be able to equip myself with a lot more experience.

II

The Mercedes contract specified the Grandes Epreuves and four sports car events: the Mille Miglia, Le Mans, the Nurburg 1,000 kilometres, and Pan-Americana, which was quite a plateful, having regard to the fact that I was "free" to drive British cars in other events. The car I had tried out at Hockenheim was, as I have said, no prototype; indeed, it was No. 8 model of a modified car with shorter chassis than the Mercedes we had seen. Seven cars already were on their way to the Argentine for the two big races which opened the International calendar early in the New Year.

There I followed, to undertake my first two engagements with the car. What an extraordinary contrast with my activities a year before! In January 1954, I was slithering down the icy slopes of the Alps in the Monte Carlo Rally; this year I was sweltering in heat which knocked the stuffing out of one, heat which made it an effort to move. It was worst on the day of the Argentine Grand Prix, or, to give its official title, the Gran Premio de la Republica Argentina.

There had been considerable jockeying for positions on the starting grid during the practice periods, which drew enormous crowds of Argentinians, all fervently and excitedly cheering their heroes, Fangio and Gonzales. Both these great drivers won their way to the first line on the grid, and what a line-up it was: Ascari (Lancia); Fangio (Mercedes); Gonzales (Ferrari) and Behra (Maserati)! Four different makes in premier positions. I was No. 1 in the third line, and yet my best practice time was less than a second slower than that of Ascari and Fangio who had dead-heated for positions 1 and 2.

138

The Argentine autodrome was a short, twisty one of just under 2¼ miles, but it accommodated about a quarter of a million people. In the blistering heat, which was well over 130 degrees on the circuit, the start was really terrific, with half a dozen of us snarling away in a fight for the lead. To the delight of the crowd, Fangio and Gonzales whipped away from the start with Ascari, Farina and myself close up, but by the first turn Ascari had roared by Gonzales and I had managed to pass the great Farina. After three laps, Ascari had gone by Fangio, and Gonzales and I were still chasing them with only a fraction of a second between the lot of us.

A multiple crash eliminated three or four drivers, including Behra and Karl Kling of our Mercedes team. It was a case of musical chairs for lap after lap, with the lead repeatedly changing hands between Gonzales, Fangio and Ascari. We were all feeling a little groggy on that twisty course which called for so much work in such torrid heat. Ascari skidded on an oil patch and crashed without seriously hurting himself; then Gonzales went into the pits almost on the point of collapse from fatigue, and there was a deal of driver swopping in the Ferrari camp.

At thirty laps, I was lying second to Fangio when a complete vapour lock caused me to stop way out on the circuit. Barely had I come to a halt than I was completely surrounded by well intentioned, gesticulating ambulance men. Here, thought they, was another victim of the heat; the poor driver, he has the sunstroke. The more I waved and shouted and protested the more I aroused their pity. They thought I was light-headed, and no wonder; I was not responsible for my actions; and all the time I was fighting to get back to my car and away from the clutches of these ambulance boys. Never did the tie of tongues serve me a worse trick. I was hot, of course, but not overcome.

In complete despair at not being able to explain, I found myself thrust into an ambulance. Every time I sat up to remonstrate they pushed me down again. It was not until we caught up with an interpreter, on our way to hospital, that I was able to escape and get to the pits. There I took over Hermann's car and finished fourth, but it seemed a bit tough to be taken away from a race just because I couldn't speak the lingo and looked dead-beat.

The race was a great physical triumph for the mighty Fangio. He drove the same car throughout, and averaged over 80 miles an hour for over 200 miles in conditions which had prostrated many drivers and ruined many engines. It took no fewer than three drivers to bring home the second car, a Ferrari, driven by Gonzales, Farina and Trintignant in turn, and three more drivers, Farina, Maglioli and Trintignant, to secure third place on another Ferrari. Both Kling and Hermann had driven for periods in the car on which I crossed the line. Never before, in any race, had there been so much inter-changing of drivers; but standing out in supreme and solo glory was Juan Fangio.

A fortnight later we all met in another Grand Prix, which was included in the great festival of speed at Buenos Aires. This was, again to give it its national title, the Gran Premio de la Ciudad de Buenos Aires. The circuit was altered to include an even twistier section. The conditions of the event were rather novel in that there were two heats, and the winner was he who achieved the fastest overall time for both heats.

This time, practice had given me a place in the front line with Fangio, Trintignant and Gonzales, and I was able to win the preliminary sprint, to be passed quite soon by Fangio. There I drove behind the master, with Karl Kling bringing up third place. But the Ferraris weren't going to lie down to another German victory if they could help it. Farina was given the all-out signal, and in a superb demonstration of driving skill he passed all three of us to lead at twenty of the thirty laps. Despite all that Fangio and I could do —and once we actually did pass Farina again—the Italian stormed into the lead and finally won a very great race by just over ten seconds from Fangio and myself. But that was only the first leg of the two-pronged race. It should be mentioned here that we had extra hard tyres fitted for the heat and they were not really satisfactory. They were changed for the second heat and the difference was enormous.

Before the second heat there was another quite considerable interchange of drivers. Gonzales did not start, though he had been well up in the first heat, and his car was taken over by Trintignant, whose car, in turn, was driven by Maglioli. Fangio and I went off together in the second heat, but where was Farina? He made a bad start, spun round in the first lap and drove into the pits to hand his car over to Gonzales, whose hopeless quest was to make up a lap on our Mercedes cars, which were well out in the lead.

I played follow-my-leader to Fangio; but just when it seemed that we were going to have an easy time of it, Trintignant drew closer and closer. Bigger and bigger, the Trintignant Ferrari was imaged in my driving mirror, but I never did like being the middle of a sandwich in a race, so I put my foot down. I passed Fangio, and there I stayed to the end, to finish three seconds ahead of him. I had come third in the first heat and first in the second, while Fangio had finished second in each. On aggregate time, Fangio was just about 30 seconds the better, so we were placed first and second, which wasn't at all a bad performance. The Mercedes people must have been quite delighted at taking the Argentinian G.P., and then finishing first and second in the Buenos Aires G.P.

There was no doubt at all about the supremacy of the Mercedes, and the organisation was superb. In the few minutes which elapsed between the two heats in the Buenos Aires race, the pit boys had carved holes in all sorts of places on the car so as to secure as much cooling as possible.

Looking back on that trip to the Argentine, I can almost feel myself sweating now—and it is winter in England as I write this. But there were highlights and fun. There was the time, for example, when, driving to the circuit to have a look-see before practice, with Hans Hermann at the wheel, we hit a small van and rather bashed my side of the car. Not a lot of damage, but we didn't want Neubauer to know about it, so we had it repaired overnight and got away with it. Whenever we went out with Fangio, we found ourselves shining in the reflected glory of a national hero, for he was acclaimed wherever he went.

On the night following the two-heat Buenos Aires race, I just couldn't sleep a wink, which may have been due to the pill the doctor gave me between the two races, or just to sheer exhaustion—over-tiredness. But, my goodness, was it hot! During the second heat of that race, even the chewing-gum melted in my pocket.

During the fortnight between the two Grand Prix races, we were invited to meet President Perón. He had an interesting collection of models in his room; two tractors, a Stratocruiser, a stuffed toad and a great and ugly-looking vulture.

I wasn't sorry to leave the feverish heat of the Argentine, though, by contrast, it was mighty cold in England after the flight back.

III

At the end of February I flew away again, this time to Nassau and the States for the Sebring race where, in conformity to a pre-arranged agreement, I was to drive an Austin Healey with Lance Macklin as co-driver. I had a really wonderful time there, with spear fishing and water ski-ing galore in my leisure hours. I also played golf, at which I am not very expert. My most enjoyable times were when ski-ing behind a fast boat.

On the Sebring circuit they have the quaintest ideas of safety-first, and they really must do something to mend their ways for an event which ranks in the World Competition for the Sports Car Championship. During the dark hours of the race an official quietly proceeded in the reverse direction of the track with only his sidelights on. An ambulance van whose crew were attending to a driver who had crashed was left in the middle of the track just after a blind corner. There seemed to be little attempt to prevent spectators from wandering across the track, and you don't really expect the official in charge of the pits to drive up and down them in his own private car.

The race itself was a triumph for Mike Hawthorn and his co-driver Phil Walters on a D type Jaguar, leading practically throughout to average 79·3 m.p.h. for the entire twelve hours. We didn't do at all badly, finishing sixth in general classification and fourth in the "Index of Performance" register. The Ferrari people immediately lodged a protest against the winning Jaguar, and there were all sorts of other protests, but after some delay the officials announced that the protests had not been upheld.

I had thoroughly enjoyed nearby Nassau, especially the spear fishing and water ski-ing, and this time, when I got back to England, there were signs of the coming spring, fore-runner of what was to be the finest summer, both from the point of view of weather and motoring achievements, that I had ever experienced.

With a few days to spare before the season really started, I tried to relax, seeing films, plays, etc., in London. I took the Maserati to Silverstone to do a bit of experimental work, and made several adjustments to the brakes. Soon I was on the Continent again. Why? Mere thoroughness.

The Mille Miglia was on its way round again, and the Mercedes crowd were very anxious to win it, which meant practising on the circuit for the drivers. For some time, therefore, I found myself learning all I could of the Brescia–Rome–Brescia course. Neubauer is a stickler for work, but he has his sense of humour as well. He once said: "My secretary is too old, she is sixty, I shall have to change her for three of twenty!"

On April 1st—another item in the superstition register—I was up at the crack of dawn for a run from Brescia in a 300 SL. I averaged 78 miles an hour to Ravenna, and was going well when a military truck (bombs aboard) pulled directly across me and, without the slightest chance of avoiding it, I crashed. I broke the model rather badly, but escaped injury. That period of practice was to serve me well, as the story of the Mille Miglia that year will disclose.

When the Mercedes people were content that we had done enough I went back to London and worked.

Easter Monday saw the first International meeting of the season, at Goodwood. Not a very good meeting for me. The big race was the Formula 1 event for the Richmond Cup, a 21-lapper (50 miles) in which I drove the Maserati. It felt awful, due to the fact that it had the wrong wheels on, and though I led for thirteen laps, the fuel pump then failed. The dashing Salvadori recovered from a spin round on the track, and won. I had the same trouble with the Maserati in the open formula race and could only finish third, while, to complete my discomfiture, my Climax engined car in the 1½-litre race blew up. It was Badwood, not Goodwood, that day.

(*Right*): A scene during the 1956 Rheims 12-hour race when Stirling drove his Cooper Climax 1500 c.c. sports car with Phil Hill. Mechanic Alf Francis deals with the oil; friend Lionel Leonard deals with the water, whilst Stirling puts in the petrol. The car eventually retired with over-heating troubles.

(*Left*): Stirling has a Coca-Cola after his victory in the Governor's Trophy Race, Nassau, 1956, with a 3-litre Maserati. Bill Lloyd, the car's owner, looks reflective; perhaps he is remembering his and Stirling's win in the Sebring 12-hour race, 1954, with the Briggs Cunningham - owned and entered OSCA. (*Photo: Tom Burnside*)

(Above): Stirling in the *Daily Express* Trophy Race, 1956, which event he won driving the British-built Vanwall. It was partly as a result of his excellent impressions of the car during this race that he later signed on to drive for Mr. Tony Vandervell during 1957. *(Photo: T. C. March)*

(Below): Stirling in his new Healey ski-boat off Nassau, Bahamas, during the Bahamas Speed Week. His passenger is Mrs. Peter Collins. *(Photo: Leo Patrick Cummings)*

(*Above*): With the Vanwall at Goodwood, April 1957, at the start of the Richmond Trophy Race. Note the smoke pouring from the offside rear tyre as the spinning wheel literally burns the rubber off.
(*Photo: M. E. S. Compton*)

(*Right*): In Rouen with Peter Collins on an unusual form of transport. (*Photo: Kemsley*)

(Left): With Bambi, the giant stuffed animal Stirling purchased in Buenos Aires and brought home with him much to the amusement of the airline and his fellow passengers.

(Right): A superb shot of Stirling the water-skier, a sport in which he has always been intensely interested and increasingly proficient.
(Photo: Mirrorpic)

12

MILLE MIGLIA SCIENCE

I

THERE was no time to mope over these minor troubles for I was soon in the air again on my way to Brescia for more Mille Miglia practice and on to Bordeaux for the local Grand Prix. This wasn't a Grande Epreuve, and since the Mercedes policy was that their drivers should get all the practice they could, and since my contract permitted me to drive outside the Mercedes range of events, I drove the Maserati. The official Maserati team was composed of Behra, Mieres and Musso, and when, in my privately owned car, I knocked a fraction of a second off Gonzales' record, the Maserati mechanics sat up and took notice.

But it is a very difficult thing for a privately owned car to beat the works entered models, and so it proved in the race, for the three official Maserati drivers were first, with Behra winning from Musso and Mieres. I managed to win fourth place, but I had a difficult race. The acceleration was poor and the front brakes were locking. I managed to push my way up from eighth to fourth, but had to beat the lap record to do so.

Now the Mille Miglia was upon us, and back I went to Brescia to discover that Mercedes had fitted a new windscreen which, on test, proved to be an improvement.

Dawn in Brescia and the cars were all ready for the start. My passenger was Denis Jenkinson, who was to be a tower of strength and a perfect "second" in what was destined to be my greatest triumph. Ten hours and four minutes later we had won the great race, the first time an Englishman had ever done it; we had broken all records and averaged 97·9 miles an hour over that tortuous, twisty course of 1,000 miles.

Those are stark facts, but they were achieved, not by the prowess of the driver, but scientifically. It is probable that never before had so much science been applied to the preparations for a race. We had practised assiduously and had devised all sorts of second-saving ideas. Denis Jenkinson had a sort of roller map which he was able to unwind as we went along and, using it, he was able to give me hand signals so that I would know even when the road ahead was blind, either by reason of a hump-backed bridge or a corner, exactly what the hazard demanded. He was, in fact, a "second sight", and our progress throughout that 1,000 miles was a perfect demonstration of the fact that two heads are better than one. Everything to the tiniest detail was plotted not only by us but also, on the mechanical side, by the Mercedes staff.

We had full dress rehearsals, with the pits in attendance and Jenkinson perfecting his roller map and signals system. We plotted time schedules for the various stretches, basing them on a two miles an hour faster run than the record for the race. Races, many races, have been won by flukes; many more have been won by sheer driving ability, but the Mille Miglia of 1955 was won on a pattern of complete co-ordination and planning.

II

We went off, running down the ramp and into the close-packed streets of Brescia . . . but here is Denis Jenkinson for his report of the event in a series of extracts from his descriptive story in *Motor Sport*:

"Before starting" [writes Jenkinson] "I had a complete

list of our more serious rivals and also the existing record times to every control point round the course. We had privately calculated on an average of 90 m.p.h.—two miles an hour over the Marzotto record. Mercedes gave us no orders, leaving the running of the race entirely to each driver, but insisting that the car was brought back to Brescia if it were humanly possible.

"Stirling and I made a pact that we would keep the car going as long as practicable, having decided at which point we could have the engine blow up and still coast in to the finish, and how many kilometres we were prepared to push it to the finish or to a control. There were Mercedes pits at Ravenna, Pescara, Rome, Florence and Bologna, completely equipped with everything that might be required. The enormous entry—over 500—had begun to leave Brescia while we were tucked up in bed at 9 p.m. on the night previous to our departure, but the winner would, of course, come from among the late starters in the early hours of the next morning.

"Starting positions were arranged by ballot, and this was quite important, for the later starters had the advantage of knowing what was going on ahead of them. They could, at their pits, secure exact information of the times of their rivals, while the early starters in the fast group could not tell what was going on behind them and had to be a jump ahead for real information. For example, with Taruffi, a greatly fancied driver, starting later than us, we would have to wait until Pescara before we could know our relative positions at Ravenna.

"Among the important men who started ahead of us were Fangio and Kling on Mercedes S.L.R.s like ours, Peter Collins (Aston Martin) and a group of Ferraris headed by Maglioli. Our big worry was not so much those ahead as those behind. Thirty seconds before our starting time, 7.22 a.m., Moss started the engine, which roared into life and then, as the flag fell, we were off to a surge of acceleration and

147

up to peak revs. in first, second and third gears, weaving our way through the vast crowds.

"We had the sun shining full in our eyes, which made navigating difficult, but I had written the notes over and over again and gone over the route so many times in my imagination that I almost knew it by heart. One of the first signals was to take a gentle S-bend through a village on full throttle in fourth gear, and as Moss did this, being quite unable to see the road for more than 100 yards ahead, I settled down to the job, confident that our scientific method of equalling the Italians' ability in open-road racing was going to work.

"At no time before the race did we contemplate getting into the lead, for we fully expected Fangio to set the pace with Kling determined to win at all costs; we were out for a third place to beat the Ferraris out of it.

"On the straights to Verona we were getting 7,500 revs. in top gear, which meant about 170 m.p.h. On some of these long straights our navigation system was paying handsomely, for we could keep at 170 over blind hillbrows, even when overtaking slower cars. Moss, sure in the knowledge that all he had to do was to concentrate on keeping the car on the road, was travelling as fast as possible. This in itsel was more than enough, but he was sitting back in his usual relaxed position, making no apparent effort, until some corners were reached, when the speed at which he controlled slides, winding the wheel from right to left and back again, showed that his superb reflexes and judgment were on top of their form.

"Approaching Padua, Moss pointed behind and I looked round to see a Ferrari gaining on us rapidly and, with a grimace of disgust at one another, we realised that it was Castellotti. The Mercedes was giving all it had, and Moss was driving hard but taking no risks, letting the car slide just so far on the corners and no more. Entering the main street of Padua at 150 m.p.h., we braked for the right-angle bend at the finish and suddenly I began to realise that Moss was beginning to work furiously on the steering wheel, for we were arriving at the corner much too fast and it seemed doubtful whether we could stop in time.

"I sat fascinated, watching Moss working away to keep control, and I was so intrigued to follow his every action that I completely forgot to be scared. With the wheels almost on locking point, he kept the car straight to the last possible fraction of a second, making no attempt to get round the corner, for that would have meant a complete spin and anything could have happened. Just when it seemed we must go head-on into the straw bales, Moss got the speed down low enough to risk letting go the brakes and try taking the corner. As the front of the car slid over the dry road, we went bump into the bales with our left-hand front wing, bounced off into the middle of the road, and as the car was then pointing in the right direction, Moss selected bottom gear and opened out again.

"All this time Castellotti was just behind us, and as we bounced off the bales he nipped by us, grinning over his shoulder. As we set off after him, I gave Moss a little handclap of appreciation. Through Padua we followed the Ferrari, and on acceleration we could not hold it, but the Italian was driving like a maniac, sliding all the corners, using the pavement and the loose edges of the road. Round a particularly dodgy left-hand bend on the outskirts of the town I warned Moss and then watched Castellotti sorting out his Ferrari, the front wheels on full understeer with the inside one off the ground and rubber pouring off the rear tyres, leaving great white marks on the road. This was to watch motor racing from the best possible position, and beside me was a quiet, calm young man who was following the Ferrari at a discreet distance, ready for any emergency.

"Out of the town we joined an incredibly fast stretch of road, straight for many miles, and we started alongside the Ferrari in bottom gear; but try as we might, the red car drew away from us, and once more Moss and I exchanged puzzled looks. By the time we had reached our maximum speed the Ferrari was over 200 yards ahead, but there it remained, the gap being preserved during the whole length of the straight. At the cut-off point at the end, we gained considerably, both from the fact that we knew exactly when the following left-hand corner was approaching and also from slightly superior brakes. More full-throttle running saw us keeping the Ferrari in sight and then, as we approached a small village, we saw Castellotti nip past another Ferrari while we were held up in the village street.

"Even so, Castellotti remained in sight, and after a wave to Peter Collins, who had broken down just before Rovigo, we went into the town at terrific speed. Straight across the square we went, where in practice we had to go round the island; broadside we left the last right-hand turn in the town, with the front wheels on full opposite lock and the throttle pedal hard down. Castellotti was a little nearer, but out on the open roads he was driving so near the limit that on every corner he was throwing up the gravel from the road verge. This sent up a huge cloud of dust, and we could never be sure whether or not we were going to enter it to find the Ferrari sideways across the road or bouncing off the banks and trees.

"No sort of scientific approach to the matter could cope with this sort of hazard. Wisely, Moss dropped back a little and the Ferrari got ahead of us, sufficiently to let the dust settle. On we went to Ravenna and all along the way there were signs of people having the most almighty incidents, black marks from locked wheels making the weirdest patterns on the roads, and many times, on corners we had marked as dangerous or dodgy, we came across cars in the touring categories, lying battered and bent by the roadside, sure indication of the fact that our grading of the corners was not far wrong.

"To Ravenna, the road winds a good deal, and now I could admire the Moss artistry as he put in some very steady 'nine-tenths' motoring, especially round open bends that he could see or knew. Approaching the Ravenna control I took the route-card board from its holder, held it up for Moss to see, to indicate that we had to stop here to receive the official stamp and then, as we braked towards the 'Controllo' banner across the road, I held my right hand well out of the car to indicate to the numerous officials which side we wanted the official with the rubber stamp to be. Holding the board on the side of the cockpit, we crossed the control line, bang went the rubber stamp, and we were off without having to come to rest. Just beyond the control there was a row of pits, and there was Castellotti's Ferrari having some tyre changes, which was not at all surprising.

"Moss yelled 'Castellotti' to draw my attention to what I had already seen, and we twisted our way through the streets of Ravenna, nearly collecting an archway in the process, and then out on the fast winding road to Forli. Our time to Ravenna had been very fast, but Castellotti had passed us and got there before us, and we had no idea how Taruffi and the others behind us were doing.

"Ever since leaving the start, we had had the rising sun shining in our eyes and what with the body sway, the heat from the gear-box by my left buttock, the engine fumes and the nauseating brake-lining smells, my stomach cried 'enough' and what little breakfast I had eaten went overboard, together with my spectacles, for I made the mistake of turning my head sideways at 150 m.p.h. with my goggles lowered.

"Fortunately I had a spare pair, and there was no time to worry about a protesting stomach, for we were approaching Pesaro, where there was a sharp right corner. Now the blue calm Adriatic appeared on our left, and we were on the long coastal straights, taking blind brows and equally blind bridges at our full 170 m.p.h. I chuckled to myself as I realised that Moss was not lifting his foot, as he had threatened. It was interesting at this point to pass many of the early starters, with here and there the wreck of a car whose driver had been more daring than discreet.

"All this time, we were completely in the dark as to the progress of our more dangerous rivals, although we knew, of course, that Castellotti was somewhere behind, delayed by tyre trouble. It was a long leg to the next control at Pescara, and we were at peak speed most of the time. On one straight, lined with trees, we had marked down one hump as being 'flat out' only if the road was dry. It was, so I gave the appropriate signal and we took it at 7,500 revs. in fifth gear. For a measurable amount of time the vibro-massage you get sitting in a 300 S.L.R. at that speed suddenly ceased, and there was time for us to look at each other with raised eyebrows before we landed again. Even if we had been in the air for only one second, we should have travelled 200 feet, and I estimated the 'duration of flight' at something more than a second. The road was dead straight; the Mercedes made a perfect four-point landing, and I thankfully praised the driver because he did not move the steering wheel a fraction of an inch, for that might have been our end.

"With the heat of the sun and the long straights, we had been getting into a complacent stupor, but this little incident brought us back to reality, and we were fully on the job when we approached Pescara. Over the level-crossing we went, far faster than we had done in practice, and the car skated right across the road with all four wheels sliding. I was sure that we were going to write off some petrol pumps, but somehow Moss got control again and we merely brushed some straw bales and then braked heavily to a stop for the second control stamp.

"Here we were to make our first fuel replenishment, and as I held out the route card I pointed to the filler, but Moss was before me. Just beyond the control was the Mercedes pit, and as we pulled in, everything happened at once. Eighteen gallons of fuel went in from a gravity tank, just sufficient to get us to our main stop at Rome; the windscreen, thick with dead flies, was cleaned, the tyres were examined; we were handed a slice of orange and a peeled banana, and somebody was holding a piece of paper in front of Moss. On it was written: Taruffi, Moss, 15 secs, Hermann, Kling, Fangio.

"That told us that at the last control Taruffi was 15 seconds ahead of us in first place. Off we went to the right turn, where I saw that we were overshooting; with locked wheels we slid straight on, bang into the straw bales. I just had time to hope there was nothing solid behind the bales when the air was full of flying straw, and we were on the pavement. Moss quickly selected bottom gear and, without stopping, drove along the pavement behind the bales until we could bounce down off the kerb and proceed. Then we were switchbacking at full speed over a series of brows and so along the barren valley between the rocky mountains, to Popoli, where a Bailey bridge still serves to span the river. Along this valley I saw the strange sight of about fifty robed monks, with shining bald pates, standing on a high mound and waving to us as we went by with a noise sufficient to wake the devil himself.

"We were certainly not wasting any seconds anywhere, and Moss was driving right on the limit of adhesion all the time, sometimes over the limit, driving in that awe-inspiring narrow margin that you enter just before you have a crash, unless you have the Moss skill. Now and again we saw a train, but fortunately did not discover a level-crossing closed. But we had a remedy for it in our plans. During practice, we had tried lifting the barrier, Italian gates being two long poles that lower across the road, and found that the slack on the operating cables was just sufficient to allow the car to be driven under the pole, much to the annoyance of the crossing keeper. Anyway, the eventuality did not arise and we had a clear run all the way to Rome.

"The last six miles were an absolute nightmare. Normally we would have been doing 150 or more miles an hour, but the crowds of spectators were so thick that we had to slow down to about 130 m.p.h., and that was pretty hectic through the dense crowds. It seemed that all Rome was out to watch the race, all oblivious of the danger of a high-speed racing car. The last mile into the control was better organised, and we went into the control without trouble. Down came the stamp on the control card, and we were into the Mercedes pits, with our engine switched off for the first time since we had left Brescia. We had barely stopped when the car was jacked up, the rear wheels changed, the fuel tank filled and a refreshing shower of water thrown over me. A hand appeared with a piece of paper and on it I read: Moss, Taruffi, Hermann, Kling, Fangio. The times showed that we had a lead of nearly two minutes.

"So we led at Rome, and Moss drove off with every intention of breaking down the superstitious tradition that whoever leads at Rome will not win at Brescia. Soon we saw Kling's car wrecked by the roadside, but this had no effect on Moss, who began to put everything he knew into his driving. I had to concentrate on this difficult section, so as to give him the right signals and warnings.

"Now there was the continual hazard of passing slower cars, and then I made what I think was my only real mistake during this remarkable and historic run. Having just given warning of a dodgy right-hand bend, I received a shower of petrol down my neck coming from the filler cap and due to surge. I looked back and in doing so missed a corner which followed quickly, without giving Moss the signal. I took a sly glimpse at Moss and there he was cornering fantastically, with an irate grin on his face. Moss had remembered the corner and had not apparently spotted the petrol. I received several more cooling douches from the petrol for a few miles, but decided to say nothing about it.

"Up the Radicofani we stormed, with the car bucking and slithering about to such an extent that I should have been frightened but for my complete faith in the masterly driving of Stirling. Previously he had been pointing to the front of the car, indicating that a brake was beginning to grab on occasions, and it happened on a sharp left-hander. Without any warning, the car spun round and there was just time to think what a desolate part of Italy this was for a breakdown when I realised that we had stopped almost in our own length and were gently sliding into the ditch. It didn't seem so bad, and looked as though we could push it out, but as I was about to get out of the car, Moss dropped into bottom gear and out she came, with a dented tail. It took us two turns into reverse before we could point the car in the right direction, and as I fiddled about with the safety-catch on the reverse position, we poked our tongues out at each other in mutual derision.

"At the Siena control, we had no idea whether we were leading or not, but we knew Taruffi was on our tail, and Moss had no thought of relaxing. He continued to drive what I think must have been the most superb race of his career, twirling the steering wheel this way and that, controlling slides with perfect judgment or alternatively provoking slides so as to make the car change direction bodily. On the winding road from Siena to Florence, physical strain began to tell on me, but I gave myself renewed energy by looking at Stirling, who was seated beside me, perfectly relaxed, working away at the steering as though we had only just left Brescia instead of having driven for nearly 700 miles in a broiling sun.

"The approaches to Florence were almost back-breaking, as we bounded and leapt over the badly maintained roads. Down a steep hill in second gear, we went into third at peak revs. making me think that it took a brave man to unleash about 300 h.p. down so steep a hill and change up while doing it. At speeds sometimes exceeding 120 m.p.h. we went through the streets of Florence, over the great river bridge, broadside across a square, over tram lines and into the control.

"Now Moss had really got the bit between his teeth; nothing was going to stop him winning, I thought; he had rather a special look of concentration on his face and I knew that one of his greatest ambitions was to do the section Florence–Bologna in one hour. The road crosses the heart of the Apennines, by way of Futa and Raticosa Passes, in about 60 miles, but it is like a Prescott hill climb all the way.

"As we got the route card stamped, again without coming to rest, I grabbed the sheet of paper from the Mercedes man at the control and it told us that we were still leading the race. Moss left Florence as though at the start of a Grand Prix, and as he looked at his wrist-watch I realised that he was out to crack the hour to Bologna. 'This is going to be fantastic!' I thought as we screamed up the hills from Florence; 'he is going to do some nine-tenths plus motoring.'

"He did, while I gave him occasional signals and leaned to the left as far as possible away from Moss, for he was going to need all the room possible for his whirling arms and for stirring the gear-lever about. Up into the mountains we screamed, occasionally passing other cars. Little did we know that we had the race in our pocket, for though we were unaware of it, Taruffi had retired way back behind us with a broken oil pump and Fangio had stopped in Florence repairing an injection pipe. We had actually overtaken Fangio on the road, but his car was hidden by mechanics and onlookers and we had not seen him.

"All the time Moss was really dicing I felt a hypnotic sensation, forcing me to live every inch of the way with him. It was probably this factor that prevented me from being frightened, for nothing ever arrived unexpectedly. I was keeping up with him mentally all the way, which I had to do if I wasn't to miss any of our route marking though, physically, I had fallen way behind him and I marvelled that anyone could drive so furiously for such a long time.

"At the top of the Futa Pass there were enormous crowds all waving excitedly, and on numerous occasions Moss almost lost the car completely as we hit patches of melted tar coated with oil and rubber from the cars ahead of us. Just over the brow of the Futa we saw a Mercedes by the roadside amid a crowd of people; it was young Hans Hermann. The car looked undamaged, so we assumed he was all right.

"Now we had to get to Brescia, I thought, and we mustn't let Taruffi overtake us—we still did not know he was out of it. On we went, up and over the Raticosa Pass, plunging down the other side in a series of slides that to me felt completely uncontrolled, but which to Moss were obviously intentional. By sheer good fortune we missed the stone parapet on the outside of the corner. Down off the mountains we raced, into the broiling heat of the afternoon, and dashing into the Bologna control at nearly 150 miles an hour. We were in and out of the control so quickly that I had no time to collect the vital news sheet from our depôt, so that we did not know how we stood in the race, nor what had happened to our rivals; but we knew we had crossed the mountains in 61 minutes and were so far ahead of the record that, to me, it seemed as though we had achieved the impossible.

"The hard part was now over, but Moss did not relax, for it had now occurred to him that it was possible to get back to Brescia in the round ten hours, which would make the race average 100 m.p.h. Up the long straights through Modena, Reggio-Emilia and Parma we went, not wasting a second anywhere, cruising at 170 m.p.h., cutting off only where I indicated corners or bumpy hillbrows. Looking up, I suddenly realised that we were overtaking an aeroplane, and then I knew I was living in the realms of fantasy; when we caught and passed a second one my brain began to boggle at the sustained speed. They were flying at about 300 feet, filming our progress, and it must have looked most impressive.

"This really was pure speed; the car was going perfectly and reaching 7,600 r.p.m. in fifth gear in places, which was as honest a 170 m.p.h. plus as I'd care to argue about. Through Cremona we went, and now we were on the last leg of the course, there being a special prize and the Nuvolari Cup for the fastest speed from Cremona to Brescia.

Although the road lay straight for most of the way, there were half a dozen villages to traverse as well as the final route-card stamp to get in the town of Mantua. In one village, less than fifty miles from the finish, we had an enormous slide on some melted tar, and for a moment I thought we would hit a concrete wall, but with that absurdly calm manner of his, Moss tweaked the wheel this way and that, caught the car just in time, and with his foot hard down we went on our way as if nothing had happened.

"The final miles into Brescia were sheer joy, and after we had passed my final direction indicator, I put my roller map away and thought: 'If it blows to pieces now, we can carry it the rest of the way.' We took the last corner into the finishing line at well over 100 m.p.h., still not knowing that we had made motor history, but happy and contented at having completed the race. On the way to the official car park, Stirling said: 'Do you think we've won?' To which I replied: 'We must wait for Taruffi to arrive, and we don't know when Fangio got in.'

"We were soon informed that we had actually won, and we clasped each other in delirious joy. Then we were swept away amid a horde of police and officials. Our total time for the course was 10 hours 7 minutes 48 seconds, an average of nearly 98 m.p.h. From Cremona to Brescia we had averaged 123 m.p.h. As we were driven back to our hotel, tired, filthy, oily and covered in dust and dirt, we grinned happily at each other's black faces, and Stirling said: 'I'm so happy to have proved that a Briton can win the Mille Miglia and that the legend "he who leads at Rome never leads at Brescia" is finished.'"

I quote Denis Jenkinson's story fairly fully, because it is a dramatic account of the Mille Miglia, but he does not give himself the very great credit due for his skilful and efficient navigation. He relieved me of a great deal of work, and certainly permitted me to travel far faster than I could have done with a lesser helpmate. I cannot think of anyone else in whom I would have as much faith; Denis is a remarkable man in many ways.

It is perhaps the most difficult, and possibly the most hazardous of all races, but many of the risks can be eliminated by thoroughness of preparation, and the manner in which the Mercedes staff organised both before and during the event was a complete revelation.

For the record, maybe I should add that our average with the Mercedes, officially 97·93 m.p.h., was a record since the Mille Miglia was first held, back in 1927, and remains so today. The race was suppressed after 1957, as the Marquis de Portago, his American passenger and several spectators were all killed when his Ferrari crashed on the last leg from Mantua—the year that Piero Taruffi, who had tried so hard for so many years, finally won the race.

13

DUELS WITH FANGIO

I

FOLLOWING the Mille Miglia came the international race meeting at Silverstone, but Mercedes were not engaged in this, so I drove my own Maserati. She was wayward. After putting up a fast practice lap at 96·79 m.p.h., over-heating damaged the engine too badly to permit any more racing. I tried to get another engine flown over from Italy, but couldn't. I had managed to win a place on the front row of the starting grid in the International Trophy Race, but the Maserati just continued peevish and, after ten laps, I was out of it with engine trouble.

I didn't do any better in the sports car race on a Beart-Rodgers and had ignition trouble, finishing last. It was a bit of a come-down after the Mille Miglia, but there you are; motor racing has all the ups and downs of a lift. Even Silverstone, where I normally do quite well, was a complete flop.

My next event proved a major disappointment in a most remarkable motor race. The Monaco Grand Prix was, this year, in accordance with the rota, the Grand Prix de l'Europe, and it was contested by a superb field of cars and drivers. There were plenty of thrills and spills during the practice periods, but these were completely overshadowed by incidents in the race itself.

Practically everybody of note in the racing game was engaged, and among the "stables" represented were Mercedes, Ferrari, Lancia, Maserati, Vanwall and Gordini. On

160

the first line of the starting grid were Fangio and myself on Mercedes and Ascari on a Lancia, but none of us was destined to finish.

The two miles circuit had to be covered 100 times, and on such a course the driver had to be on the alert the whole time. It is a most punishing event, both for cars and those at the wheel. Fangio and I were able to leave Ascari from the start, and the two of us went round in close company, so that quite soon we had a commanding lead. Casualties were frequent, among the earliest was the ex-world champion, Farina.

At the half distance—50 laps—we were still way out ahead of the field, then I lost my "playmate". The great Fangio had engine trouble and was out, leaving me to carry on, which I did. Then, with a mere twenty laps to go, that is to say a fifth of the race, I was suddenly trying to look through a smoke screen; I had the same trouble as Juan. Triumph turned to disaster.

Ascari, although a minute and a half behind me, came out of the tunnel not knowing I was in the pits and that he was in the lead. Before he could gather this news, he was swimming for his life in the Bay. The crowd, wild in its enthusiasm, was waving and gesticulating madly. No doubt it distracted his attention, for he hit the kerb; before he had time to recover, his Lancia with locked wheels, had plunged into the harbour where it immediately sank, though the nimble Ascari won his way clear and swam for a nearby boat.

The latter stages of the race saw Castellotti, one of the "demon" type drivers, trying hard to overhaul Trintignant, who had been driving a steady race well in the rear of the leaders. Castellotti was gaining on every lap, but in trying to do too much he achieved too little, spun round on a hairpin, and thus put an end to what looked like being an exciting pursuit race, for he lost too much time in his spin to have any chance of catching his man. So an astounding hare and tortoise race resulted in a surprising, but none the less well merited, win for Trintignant on a Ferrari. Once again it was demonstrated most clearly that in motor racing the race is not always to the swift. Trintignant won by steady driving when at least half a dozen faster men had been eliminated by mechanical trouble or accident. The result was a bitter blow for Mercedes and also for Juan Fangio, questing for the retention of his world title; but he need not have worried, for he was able to keep his title.

Quickly following the Grand Prix de l'Europe was the 18th International Eifelrennen at the Nurburgring, and here Fangio and I had one of those close struggles which were to become familiar to the racing crowds during 1955.

This was for sporting and production cars. Farina had a Ferrari which was fast but completely unmanageable. I managed to put in a record lap and did a little pacemaking for Fangio for most of the race, but he challenged in the last lap and went by the post, with me alongside, watching him. Masten Gregory drove a fine race in his 3-litre Ferrari at this race. In spite of the fact that Ferraris and Jaguars were there, this event was very much a domestic affair and attention was focused on the Belgian Grand Prix, which, as the third in the series, would determine leadership in the World Championship between Mercedes and Ferrari.

The Francorchamps circuit is just about the fastest and loveliest of all the G.P. courses, but, of course, you don't have much time to enjoy the scenery in a Grand Prix. It is roughly the shape of a triangle, with extremely fast straights, which, more than other courses, really gives you a chance of plenty of full-bore motoring. The field was not a large one, but select, though there was a painful gap in the Lancia team because Alberto Ascari, ex-world champion, had been killed during trials on the Monza track. He was a very great man, and loved by all.

There was quite a lot of jockeying with cars by the Mercedes camp during practice. Fangio had a medium-length wheelbase car with outboard front brakes; I had the same type of car but with inboard brakes, and Kling had a long chassis job which was used for training. We rang the changes on the different models. In the first practice session, Fangio put up a lap time of 4 minutes 18·7 seconds, which beat his old Alfa Romeo record by nearly 4 seconds—what a fantastic driver he is! My best time was 4 minutes 24 seconds.

The second day's practice brought something of a shock to the Mercedes. Juan Fangio got down to 4 minutes 18·2 seconds, and I managed one of 4 minutes 19·2 seconds, so it looked all right for the two silver Mercedes in the premier starting positions. But oh dear, no. Castellotti, who is really one of the most daring and courageous drivers, clipped a tenth of a second off Fangio's lap and won his right to the position at the head of the field on a Lancia. We might have managed to oust him from that position on the next and final day of practice, but the weather was shocking and destroyed our hopes. They sent me out for a practice lap on bald tyres, but the best I could do was 5 minutes 52 seconds in a circuit which frightened the life out of me. Just to add anything that was needed to give me a sort of mental upset, my own Maserati threw a connecting-rod while being run in.

At the circuit on race day I was presented to the ex-King of Belgium, and he was most charming. It was an excellent day, and the roads leading to the circuit were crammed with people. Down went the flag, with Fangio roaring past Castellotti, and me following the wheel tracks of the master, so that in 500 yards we were first and second. Fangio neatly flicked his car into the first corner, thus effectively preventing Castellotti from sneaking through on the inside, and at the end of the first lap it was Fangio 1; Moss 2; and with both of us detached from the field.

On lap 15, approaching half-way, Fangio put up a new lap record of 4 minutes 20·8 seconds; not quite so fast as the best practice lap, but then practice laps do not count as records. Then he put up another record at an average of about 121 m.p.h. I was driving comfortably behind the leader and when he began to ease up, with the discretion of the really great driver who knows the race is in his pocket, I closed up on him. Our nearest competitor was Farina, but he was nearly two minutes behind and the closing stages of the race were more like a demonstration run with Fangio and myself well away.

Finally, Fangio won easily by 8 seconds at 118·72 m.p.h. Young Paul Frere, the Belgian, drove a fine race in a Ferrari to which he was not accustomed, to finish fourth behind Farina; as for Castellotti, he held off the challenge of Farina for third place for 15 laps and then blew up his car. He is a magnificent driver, but inclined to cane his horses. So the stigma of Monte Carlo, where the Mercedes had failed badly, was completely wiped out. Fangio was well on the way to another World Championship, and the Germans had resumed their domination of the racing game.

The following week-end was Le Mans. What a terrible tragedy occurred, and what a shocking disaster. It is now history, very tragic history, how poor Levegh crashed into the grandstands, his Mercedes ploughing down the assembled multitude and killing over 80 people. Some time after the tragedy we withdrew from the race, when over 2 laps in the lead. The disaster was to have important repercussions throughout the racing world. Improved safety measures were adopted; France blanked her calendar entirely, and Grand Prix and other classic races were cancelled throughout Europe. It was semi-panic, and an earnest consideration of the conditions for the safety of spectators.

Racing round the circuit I did not, of course, know the full extent of the frightful accident. It would appear that it was something that wouldn't happen once in a million times, but though the casualties were dreadfully heavy—indeed, unprecedented—those poor enthusiasts did not die in vain. Motor racing will be much safer because of the terror of Le Mans. My most ghastly recollection of that frightful affair was when, a few days later, I went to Levegh's funeral. It was macabre, with film and cameramen in the church.

On the following Sunday the Dutch Grand Prix was due to be run, and though cancellations were taking place everywhere, it was decided to carry on. The organisers could hardly have done differently, with all preparations in a state of maturity.

The French Government had decided to ban all organised motoring and motor-cycling sport until new safety regulations had been approved, and Switzerland and Spain more or less agreed with their policy, while Italy, Germany and Great Britain felt that the disaster should not mean a close-down on racing, although they were just as determined to consider and adopt new safety measures.

There was some doubt for a time as to whether Mercedes would send a team to Holland; and it was not until the Dutch promoters had agreed to adopt certain safety measures that they agreed to do so. These measures included a yellow line painted on the right-hand side of the road preceding the pit area, cars coming in having to pull in to the right of this line, well clear of those passing at full speed.

The Zandvoort track is not unlike Goodwood, measuring 2·6 miles and having to be covered 100 times in what was called the Grote Prija van Nederland. In practice, the three Mercedes cars had won the front row on the starting grid with Fangio as leader, then myself, then Kling.

The terrific crowd at the start saw Fangio get clear away, in his accustomed rôle of sprinter for the lead. I made a bad start and was passed by Musso on the Maserati, but it did not take me long to re-pass him and, indeed, Kling as well, so that we were back in the old familiar pattern of Fangio leading and me trailing him round at the head of the field. This time, however, it was not the Ferraris chasing us, but the Maseratis. The former had Mike Hawthorn, Castellotti and Trintignant, but none of them could get any real speed out of their cars.

So for 100 laps Fangio led, and I was running along within a length or so of him. We were the only two to complete the century of laps, with Roberto Mieres bringing home his Maserati in third place a lap behind. Certainly the 1955 G.P.s seemed to be set to a pattern and I was getting quite accustomed to hear the band playing the Argentine Anthem while I parked my car in second place. It had come to be fairly definitely established by now that when the Mercedes kept out of trouble they were more than a match for their Italian rivals.

I was quite looking forward to the Alpine Rally, which was due to follow the Dutch G.P., but at the last moment the Automobile Club of Marseilles and Provençe, having received a communication from the French Federation, decided to abandon the event. I had been chosen as skipper of the Sunbeam Talbot team, whose cars had been well prepared and whose indefatigable manager, Norman Garrad, had made his usually thorough plans. The cancellation probably did me a bit of good, for I was able to take time off on the Riviera and have some really good water ski-ing, spear fishing and swimming. There was also plenty of dancing in the evenings, and even if I did stay up late most nights, I made up for it by rising late.

Having thoroughly enjoyed myself, I set off for Nurburg and the German Grand Prix, only to discover that this, too, had been abandoned. That meant another holiday, with the British Grand Prix as the next really big event on the list. Le Mans had certainly tied up motor racing, but there was no question about the British event being cancelled. This event represented my immediate ambition.

II

Whatever fate may have in store for me, Saturday, July 16th, 1955, must inevitably be a red letter day, a day I shall never forget. On that day I became the first Englishman to win the British Grand Prix. My association with the Mercedes had brought me greater triumphs than I had ever before enjoyed, but not even the realisation of one of my major ambitions, that of winning the Mille Miglia, could compare with my keenness to win a home Grand Prix, to take the chequered flag before a British crowd.

It was high summer, a glorious summer of long and sunny days, though the heavy cloud of cancellation lay over the Continent, with motor racing stricken by the disaster at Le Mans and the Grand Prix programme curtailed until the matter of safety had thoroughly been probed. So it was that the British event, held on the new track built round the Grand National steeplechase course, might well be the last of the year's classics.

Aintree is, relatively, a slow course, with very few opportunities of getting into top gear and lots of work with the gear-lever. When I went to Liverpool for practice, I was as fit as I have ever been. Sometimes it comes to everyone that they feel a kind of glow, induced by perfect health, so that everything is seen through the proverbial rose-coloured spectacles. That's how it was with me. There were no worries about the car; it was, as I was, in perfect condition. In practice, I had put up the fastest lap in 2 minutes 0·4 seconds, and so won premier position on the starting grid with Juan Fangio (Mercedes) and Jean Behra on a Maserati sharing the front line with me. Behind us were Kling and Taruffi on the other two Mercedes, and behind them Mieres and Simon (Maseratis) sharing the third line with Harry Schell on the first of the British cars, the Vanwall.

The day broke, with a cloudless sky and a heat haze already building up. It was to be a scorcher. There aren't many more picturesque motor race courses than that which confronted us before the start. All the stands were most colourfully packed with women in gay coloured gowns and men in white and coloured shirts. All the way round that three-mile course one saw the dense splashes of colour rippling in the sun. But for those of us on the line there was a stern job ahead. For 90 laps (270 miles) we were to engage in a fight for Britain's chief honour, with a record crowd of something like 150,000 watching us.

How did I feel on the starting line? I think I was just as calm as before; just that slight touch of apprehension as the flag went up; that tenseness, that keyed-up, slightly suffocating feeling which is dissipated as soon as the flag descends. Out of the corner of my eye I could see the dark face of Fangio, intent and formidable. The flag dropped, and the two Mercedes immediately poked their silver noses ahead of the red-nosed Maserati, to stay there until Journey's End. I was half a length ahead of the maestro as we turned the nearby bend, and precisely that distance in front when the chequered flag fell at the end of the race.

There has been a lot written and said about Mercedes' tactics in that great race. Was the new recruit permitted to cross the line ahead of the champion? Could Fangio have won if it had been so ordained at the start, or if it had been a "free for all"? Was Moss given the race, because a British victory was better propaganda than a South American one? All I can say is that nothing was arranged between the team manager and myself. Whether Fangio had any instructions or not, I do not know, but if he had, he was certainly too great a sportsman to tell me. I have mentioned before the matter of percentages and how you sometimes go off a 100 per cent psychologically. I wasn't all that confident when the British Grand Prix started; nobody could be, with Fangio and a Mercedes in the field, but I did think that the race would go to a Mercedes.

Soon it became apparent to that mighty throng of spectators that this was the case, for we ran away from the field. Fangio passed me on the first lap. Good. What could be better than have such a master as pacemaker, especially as I did not find it too difficult to keep close to him? Already we had discovered that we could spare our horses and still maintain a gap between us and the rest of the field. We played follow my leader for lap after lap, with no signals from the pit until team manager Alfred Neubauer hung out the laconic sign "PI". We had been lapping at about 87 miles an hour, and PI means Piano, i.e., take it easy. Well, we hadn't been caning our cars at all, but orders is orders, as they say in the classics, and we turned the wick down just a little.

Somewhere in the later stages I got away from Fangio by leaving him a slower car to pass just before a corner, and was out on my own, much to the delight of the spectators, whom I could sense rather than see. At 50 laps I knew—unofficially—that I was 12 seconds ahead of Fangio which I felt was pretty fair, however the slower signal was put out once again, and I had to slow up. In the 88th lap I beat the lap record and Fangio was very, very near. Another lap and he was on my tail.

He did not catch me, but don't ask me if he could have done. When we crossed the line, his nose was about level with my steering wheel and I had won my greatest triumph after one of my most comfortable races. Never, at any time, did the car give me the slightest qualm. How happy I was when Fangio came up and congratulated me as I sat, grimy and oily, with the laurel wreath of victory round my shoulders.

It was the crowning glory to a season of triumph. Motor racing is an exacting sport. It means hard work and privations, but it offers you moments of superlative joy, such a moment as that when my foot eased off the accelerator after I had crossed the line and achieved another of my long cherished ambitions.

My average speed for the entire race was 86·47 miles an hour, but I am quite sure that if Fangio and I had been pushed harder, it could have been much higher. The speed of a winner in any big event is determined by the speed of the opposition, and though there was only half a length between the two leaders at the finish, it should be realised that Fangio and I had set a safe pacemaking trail, always preserving a margin between us and the rest of the field. Quite frankly, the opposition was not strong. The only man who could keep up with us was Jean Behra, and when he had shot his bolt it became practically a walk-over for the silver cars of Germany. Seldom had there been such a clean sweep for one "marque", for Karl Kling and Piero Taruffi brought home the other Mercedes in third and fourth positions.

III

My contract with Mercedes was for a year, with options, and I looked forward to a lengthy and productive period of racing with these superb racing cars; but soon there came a violent shock. Mercedes announced their complete withdrawal from the racing game. I was glad not to have known, in that moment of triumph, that I should no longer or, at any rate, for only a little longer, be privileged to drive a car which had placed my feet firmly on the top rungs of the ladder. It had not only been my most successful year, but also the one that had taught me most. I may have been a promising pupil but what a teacher was world champion Juan Fangio! I have many people to thank, but none more than the world champion from South America.

The next week was relatively quiet and alternated between doing some work, seeing shows and some pictures, and submitting to the demands of camera and film men. But, having been offered a Porsche in the 1,500 c.c. sports car race that preceded the Portuguese Grand Prix at Lisbon, I flew there.

The 550 Porsche just didn't fit me, the seat being too big, but it didn't take long to produce a "tailor made" cockpit. A few practice laps were reassuring. The car was quite fast, and worked up to 7,000 revs. on the straight for a speed of 190 kilometres an hour. There seemed to be a tendency for the brakes to lock, otherwise I felt quite happy about the car. The race was on the Saturday, and though I did not make too good a start, due to over-revving on an unfamiliar car, I was able to run into the lead and stayed there to the end of the race to win the Governor of Lisbon's Cup at 80·98 m.p.h.

On to the Nurburgring for practice, trying out various cars in company with Fangio and others—just another example of Mercedes thoroughness, to have their drivers testing and practising in between races. The record for the circuit has stood since 1939 when Lang did a lap in 9 minutes 43·2 seconds, but both Juan and I put in laps quicker than this. For several days we did our stuff on the Ring, then I flew back just in time to get to the Crystal Palace for a meeting.

Here I had the unusual experience of watching my own car win. I had arranged for Mike Hawthorn to drive my Maserati in the chief event, but in fact I got to the Palace in time to start the big race. This was decided in two heats and a final, and Mike had beaten the lap record in his heat. He did even better in the final, running away from Harry Schell on the Vanwall and Roy Salvadori on another Maserati, while I took pictures of them rushing round on their sixteen laps. Mike's best lap was 1 minute 3·6 seconds for an average 78·93 and a record. The Maserati had been a fickle jade during the season, but there was no doubt about its potentialities.

A few days later I went up to Bourne and later to Folkingham for a look-see at the rejuvenated B.R.M., and there again was that latent urge to drive it.

Next, off to Sweden for the sports car Grand Prix at Kristianstad. A preliminary survey of the course showed us that it was a bit narrow in places and bumpy enough here and there to give one an occasional "Journey Into Space". It is about four miles in length, and is quite interesting. Sweden was more or less a newcomer to first-class motor racing, and the promoters were taking no risks. The course was rendered as safe as possible for the spectators, who were kept well away from the circuit.

During practice, in which I won pole position for the start, I had a really funny experience. I overshot a corner and while doing everything I could to stop the car, air brakes, foot brakes, feet and everything, a policeman stood in front of me and put his hand up. Some traffic cop!

Well, the race followed the same old pattern. I took advantage of my position as No. 1 for the echelon start, and got away very well indeed; then I waved Fangio on and it was another case of follow my leader to the end with the rest of the field outpaced. We crossed the finishing line after 130 miles of racing, within one-tenth of a second of each other, our speed being just over 100 m.p.h. Sounds quite uneventful, doesn't it? It was far from it.

I had one narrow escape, for while travelling at well over 2 miles a minute a stone flew up from the road, smashed my goggles and sent some glass splinters into my left eye. I was able to withstand the shock, but mainly because the stone also hit the frame as well as the glass. I must have looked a bit gruesome, with blood running down my face, and the pain was severe, though, as is always the case, dulled a little by the excitement of racing. As soon as the race was over I went off to hospital, where fragments of glass were removed from my eye. The cars driven by Fangio and myself were identical with those we had driven at Le Mans, and were equipped with flap-like air brakes. I felt quite all right and, in fact, went to a dinner-dance the same evening.

That escape was shortly to be followed by another, but not on the race track. It happened in London at the junction of Cromwell Road and Earls Court Road while taking a friend home after a night out. These things happen suddenly, and as I took evasive action I received an almighty biff from a saloon car. The Mercedes 300 SL the factory had lent me ended up on the pavement facing the opposite way to the line of travel. My passenger escaped with a bump on the head and I bruised my elbow; the driver of the other car was luckily only slightly hurt. I reported to the police station and was eventually exonerated from blame. My bruised elbow did not prevent me from going to Snetterton, but my eye began to trouble me and the night before the race I had it checked by a doctor.

My Maserati had another off day, and nothing I could do permitted me to offer a challenge to the two Vanwalls, driven by Harry Schell and Ken Wharton, who finished first and second, with me bringing home the Maserati in third place. Subsequent examination revealed that a plug electrode had dropped into No. 1 cylinder—and it was Saturday the 13th; note the day of the month.

The following Saturday, the Goodwood Nine-Hour Race —a sort of miniature Le Mans—came round again with me sharing a Porsche with Hushke von Hanstein. Practice showed that the car was very over-geared. Race day was disappointing, with only a moderate crowd. Are long-distance races as popular as the more normal series of races that usually constitute a Goodwood programme?

The Porsche ran extremely well, and when I took over from von Hanstein just before 10 p.m., after 7 hours' racing, we were well in the running for the class award, but I hadn't been at the wheel long before Tony Crook's Cooper Bristol spun at Woodcote Corner on some oil and I could do nothing about it; I rammed him and damaged the front of the Porsche to such an extent that it could not go on, so we were out of the race with less than two hours to go. Were the gremlins coming back? A cut eye in Sweden, a road crash to follow; a Maserati mess-up at Snetterton, and now this.

Off to Monza the next day for more practice with the Mercedes. The new track is a bit bumpy and dodgy and, after a little lappery on it, we put in some fast work on the old track.

I was to have driven a Mercedes 300 SL in the International Race at Oulton, on the following Saturday, but the car was not ready in time, and I gratefully accepted the offer of Les Leston to take over Peter Bell's 1½-litre Connaught. This was very much smaller than the Aston Martins, Ferraris, Jaguars and what have you, but there was always a chance of winning the 1,500 c.c. class. I raced a Standard Ten in the *Sporting Life* Trophy in a field whose cars seemed strangely out of place in a track race. There was a Renault, a Morris Minor, a couple of Standard Tens, a Ford Consul and a whole host of cars rarely associated with the race track. I made a bad start owing to vapourisation and was never in the hunt, to finish fifth and second in my class to a D.K.W.

I made a much better start with the Connaught in the *Daily Herald* Trophy event. I was at the rear of the starting grid side but away I went along the pit counter. It was decidedly uncomfortable in the unaccustomed cockpit, but I didn't do so badly to finish seventh in a race well won by Reg Parnell on an Aston Martin; I did in fact win our class by quite a margin, at over 78 m.p.h.

Back to Aintree, with its most pleasant memories, but this time with my Maserati to contest the Formula 1 race in a programme of five events. I put up the fastest practice laps, and so won premier position on the grid. It didn't do me much good though because Reg Parnell quickly passed me on the Connaught, and I just couldn't catch him. I chased him around, quite close up, for fifteen laps; then the model began to smoke and the horses to disappear, so I retired. It looked a certainty for Parnell, but his Connaught blew up and he had to push the car over the line to finish in sixth place. Roy Salvadori won on his Maserati, being followed home by Bob Gerard, now quite a veteran, in his smaller Cooper Bristol. The best feature of the meeting was the triumph of the B.R.M.—it was one of the old type blown 1½-litre models—in the Formula Libre race, well driven by Peter Collins at over 85 m.p.h.

174

14

THE TRUTH ABOUT THE B.R.M.

A YOUNG, ambitious boy in his teens shivered on a
disused aerodrome, but soon forgot that he was cold
and a little miserable. Although he had a year's
racing behind him and could point to a few minor successes,
he was now among the *cognoscenti*; around him were some
of his boyhood heroes. They were grouped around a low-
built, sleek-looking green car. It had taken two years to
build.

Theoretically it was a wonder car, with sixteen little
cylinders whose high-frequency power thrusts would obviously give it terrific acceleration. It was in a sense, a
People's Car, but not in the sense that the description is used
today. It more or less belonged to the people because they
had subscribed to its development; they had been told that
the object of its sponsors was to smash the supremacy of the
Continental cars and show the flag on all the classic race
tracks.

The Union Jack and the chequered flag were to become
associated as never before. I listened with awe, almost
agape, as Raymond Mays told of the hopes and the confidence of the small group which, for so long, had been working on the car in the little Lincolnshire village of Bourne.
It was most impressive, and I recall the kaleidoscope of
thoughts that passed through my mind. I conjured up
visions of driving such a car. Not yet, of course, but
perhaps when I had had more experience. Then came the
unforgettable moment when Raymond Mays, running a high

175

temperature through excitement and anxiety, slid into the cockpit to give the first demonstration of what the car could do.

But the B.R.M., even in its babyhood, was temperamental. For a little while she refused to start; then came a mighty burst of noise; not a raucous bellow; not a scream, but a gloriously melodious anthem of power, the like of which had never before been played on the exhaust-pipes of a racing car. That song of power was to enthral the crowd at many a race meeting, but not often as a song of triumph. Mays drove round the track for several laps, not at any really impressive speed, but with most impressive noise. I think I was a little haunted by that noise; that vast crescendo as Mays dabbed on the acelerator. I know that I thought about the car all the way back to London, and kept thinking about it.

The idea was to give the B.R.M. a demonstrative début at the British Grand Prix in the following year at Silverstone, so that, on a home track, it would inaugurate what was to be a triumphant assault on foreign predominance. King George VI and the Queen were to be present; so was the B.R.M., but not as a competitor. It had turned sour on its designers and mechanics; it was so bug-ridden that it could not be prepared in time for the race. Instead, it ambled around the track in a demonstration run and was later put into a special enclosure in the paddock, so that their Majesties could inspect it.

In the spring of that year (1950) I had done rather well, mostly on 500 c.c. machines, and had competed in the curtain-raiser prior to the Grand Prix. Having won my heat, I finished second in the final after a close finish; but the B.R.M. was in the paddock and I had thoughts for nothing else. I went to examine it. Raymond Mays saw me and, because I had then become a promising driver, he invited me into the enclosure. There I feasted my eyes on what I still regarded as a potential world-beater.

Silverstone came round again the next August, and I was to race against the B.R.M. on an H.W.M.; against three of them, in fact. The practice days arrived—no B.R.M. On the day before the race, a London evening paper came out with the categorical statement that the B.R.M. would not start. Pandemonium. Its appearance had been boosted for weeks; its chances had been canvassed throughout the Press and the biggest ever crowd was expected to see it score a notable victory.

The fact was that there really wasn't a B.R.M. fit to race but, rather than disappoint the public, it was decided that at all costs at least one B.R.M. must face the starter. It did, but it did not start. The journalist who had most emphatically stated that it would not race saw it passing over his hotel as he had breakfast on the morning of the race on a last-minute flight in a freighter plane. He must have been a bit worried.

The late Raymond Sommer was to drive it and, as a special concession, he was given a little practice time before the first race. He qualified, but was at the back of the starters on the grid when the starting flag went down. We all thought the same thing. Would "Britain's Greatest Racing Car", as it was called in a booklet published for the meeting, do its stuff? Down went the flag, and we were off. At the end of the first lap I saw it at the track side; silent and impotent. As soon as Sommer had let in the clutch, the transmission had broken. More than 100,000 people saw their idol fail; probably only one man breathed a sigh of relief, the daring journalist who had committed himself.

II

In the winter of that year my father was approached by Raymond Mays, with a view to my driving the car in the future. So it had come already! Within a year. We had many "conversations" during the winter of 1950–1951, but not until the middle of the racing season did I finally decide to link up with the ill-fated car.

It happened after the British Grand Prix of 1951, again at Silverstone. Reg Parnell and Peter Walker were aboard B.R.M.s, and they finished the 260 mile race in fifth and seventh positions behind a fleet of Ferraris and Alfa Romeos. But they had completed a long-distance race, and they would undoubtedly have done even better had not both drivers been severely burned, owing to bad cockpit ventilation and insulation. They carried on, in great pain. The B.R.M. performance gave no occasion for complacence, but certainly built up a wave of greater confidence.

Following the race I decided to try out the B.R.M., and a little later went for testing to Folkingham, that same aerodrome where first I had marvelled at the car. On the whole, the car delighted me, but the track was not really suitable for "giving it the works", and I asked Raymond Mays to let me "have a go" at Silverstone or Goodwood. My first trial runs showed that the car needed modifications. It was more difficult to drive than any other racing car I had driven. It had a wonderful surge of power, but the whole car shuddered beneath it. In its present form, too, it prohibited the "straight-arm" position which I always use, as the cockpit was very cramped.

I was asked to sign a contract, but requested time to consider. More than anything else I wanted to drive a British car in classic races, and the only real hope of doing so with success seemed to lay in the B.R.M. So a month later, I returned to Bourne again for a long pow-wow with Raymond Mays and his technicians. I explained the position. The car was not safe. It would be necessary to alter the driving position and also get rid of the shudder and steering difficulty at speed. Mays agreed to do everything possible, and, at his invitation, I agreed to drive the car in the forthcoming Spanish Grand Prix at Barcelona. The next day I learned in the Press that I had signed on for B.R.M.s for all its races in 1952.

It was decided that the only way to get the B.R.M. into really top-notch condition was to undertake extensive trials at Monza, and to stay there until enough had been achieved. Mays wrote to say that Monza was top priority, and that the present scheme was to test to perfection and scrap all racing plans so that a real Grand Prix team could be formed for the following year.

It sounded right to me, so off I went to Monza. When I arrived Ken Richardson had just come off the track with a broken rocker arm; after this had been repaired, Ken, chief tester at Bourne, went out on a warming-up expedition— and came in after a single lap with a broken piston. That was that! I had to get back to England for racing engagements, but went back to Monza the next month.

More and more snags. A piston went again; then after a more prolonged job of "lappery" for some time, the engine started overheating. The radiator was changed, and then the engine developed a bad "period" at 9,500 revs. At last I got in a really fast lap, only a second slower than Farina's G.P. record. Things looked better until, for some obscure reason, the engine lost its revs. and instead of its 12,000 r.p.m., would not function above 10,500. We found some of the missing horses, but not all of them, and after a week or so's hard work on the track I had to return to England. The B.R.M. was still giving the mechanics headaches because of the utter unreliability of its complicated engine.

Some time later Raymond Mays declared that the tests had been eminently successful, and that he was quite sure that the next racing season would be a "B.R.M." year. But the B.R.M. Association, which was an organisation rather like a Football Supporters' Club, had lost faith; the membership had dwindled to less than half and the B.R.M. was the butt of would-be humourists. Meanwhile, I had prepared a very comprehensive report on the Monza tests in which, among other points, I stated that:

The car was difficult to steer because it became unbalanced so easily, i.e., when it was put into a slide or drift.

It had a dangerous tendency to under steering on a trailing throttle.

On fast curves, the front end of the car drifted out too far, showing that the wheels did not grip sufficiently.

The front wheels wobbled sideways, as well as the usual up and down suspension movements.

Certain structural alterations were necessary, particularly with a view to improving the driving position.

They undertook some modifications at Bourne as a result of my report, but at the end of the year, in spite of another and completely abortive trip to Monza, the B.R.M. remained a problem and, tucked away in my desk, at home, was an unsigned contract.

III

So we come to the beginning of what Raymond Mays had declared would be "the year of the B.R.M.". It started with the sensational announcement that negotiations were taking place with world champion Juan Fangio, which if finalised, would mean that he would contract to drive the B.R.M.s throughout 1952. The official notification stated: "Fangio and Moss together should prove the strongest combination ever assembled in the history of speed sport", but it was admitted that my signature was subject to the successful conclusion of track tests now proceeding.

Early in the year final tests were undertaken at Monza, and what a depressing time we had. Day after day, with nothing in the way of distractions, we plugged along in a period of alternating high speed bursts and repairs. The temperamental B.R.M. kept blowing up and losing power; but we stuck to it for weeks on end and, finally, we were satisfied that all was well. Everything was ready for the first real classic race of the year, at Turin.

It was announced that the B.R.M.s would be entered, and this was, at the time, of vital importance to all Grand Prix racing. Alfa Romeo had decided to give racing a miss in 1952, and this seemed to leave the field wide open for Ferraris. Indeed, the B.R.M.s were the only worth-while opposition. Other countries appeared anxious to promote Formula 2 races rather than Formula 1, because of the dearth of cars in the higher division, but if Ferraris and B.R.M.s put up a good show at Turin they were prepared to change their minds. If not, well, it would seem that the B.R.M.s would be deprived of the kingdom they had set out to conquer, for they were oversize for Formula 2 racing.

In order to keep the Formula 1 flag flying, the organisers of the Turin race had offered large starting money to B.R.M., even if only one car started. But it was not to be. Really hard work and concentrated attention by the mechanics had put the B.R.M.s in trim at Monza. Then came shock, dumbfounding shock. A few days before Turin, the cars and team were ordered back from Monza to England. What had happened? The B.R.M. trust had been advised that Fangio and Froilan Gonzales were on their way from the Argentine to England, and that they would arrive the day before the Turin race.

It had, in consequence, been decided to abandon Turin, because it was thought to be more important to hand the cars over to the two great Argentinians so that they could prepare to drive them in the season's G.P. races. The Monza boys were astounded. We telephoned Mays asking for permission to run at Turin; but no, the Bourne camp was completely blinded by the South American sun.

On returning to England I told Mays that I was quite prepared to play second fiddle to Fangio, so that he should have choice of car in any race we were both engaged, but that I would not sign a contract to drive exclusively for

B.R.M. Fangio and Gonzales were impressed by the car and both signed on. As a result they were commissioned to drive in the Albi Grand Prix on June 1st, a date which I could not keep because I was already engaged at Monaco. Well, Fangio and Gonzales did their stuff.

They smashed the course record, they ran away from the two 4½-litre Ferraris which were their only real challengers, and then they both blew up. A week later, the B.R.M.s were due at Dundrod for the Ulster International Race, and the Prime Minister of Northern Ireland had been told that three B.R.M.s would turn out. Why it should have been decided to race at Albi and jeopardise Irish chances, I do not know. Victory at Albi would have been a hollow one with such weak opposition, but to have done well in Northern Ireland would have been to score a notable triumph at home —and how the dwindling supporters of the car needed one.

However, two tired and insufficiently tried B.R.M.s were flown to Ireland with just enough time for a few practice laps, and Fangio and I were teamed up for the first time. I was unhappy after practice. The car tended to wander on the straights and waggle on the corners. It just wasn't safe. Mechanically it was unfit, too, for the mechanics could not get it to fire on all sixteen cylinders, and it showed signs of overheating.

Fangio reported that his car was even worse. The next morning I went to collect my car at the Belfast garage to drive it to the course. It wasn't mine. Mine had been handed over to Fangio, but nobody had told me of the switch. True, Fangio was entitled to choice of car, but why leave me in the dark? I knew the swap had been made as soon as I sat in the cockpit, but I drove to the course and arrived there with the engine nearly boiling and the clutch slipping.

When the starting flag went down, the clutch burned out and the engine stalled, and as I sat there I saw that Fangio, too, had stalled on the line. Mechanics rushed out and push-started us while the field disappeared, but with my clutch slipping badly, Fangio ran away. I met him shortly after, face to face. He had turned completely round in order to avoid a competitor he was overtaking and there he was running backwards ahead of me and nearly as fast!

The pit boys must have got a shock when I came round after the first lap, ahead of Fangio, but bigger shocks were to come. Neither of us could get round the hairpin fast enough. We had to get into bottom, under-rev. the engine, which had a very poor torque at low revs., and make up time on the straights, where we were probably the two fastest cars on the circuit. In the second lap, the gear-lever knob came off in my hand; then I had to go into the pits with over-heating trouble. Fangio couldn't get power owing to fuel starvation, so there were the two B.R.M.s—just a couple of cripples. Soon we were both out of it, and another black mark went down on the dismal history of the B.R.M.

I had had enough. I told Raymond Mays after the race that I was not keen on driving the car again. It wasn't because of the rather churlish switch of cars without telling me; I just didn't want to drive a car that frightened me. But I still had a high regard for that ill-fated car, and would have been delighted to drive it again if something could have been done about its unnerving behaviour at speed.

I should, perhaps, explain here that, when the 1,500 c.c. V16 B.R.M. was withdrawn from the race at Turin in 1952, the organizers of all the Championship Grands Prix abandoned Formula 1 in favour of Formula 2, which was open to cars with engines up to 2 litres, unsupercharged. It was hoped that there would be more entries and more competition among these machines but, in fact, Ferraris dominated the field all that season, usually led by Alberto Ascari.

The Formula 1 B.R.M. was therefore relegated to a few races open to cars of any size under Formule Libre, "Free to All". In 1954 a new Formula 1 was substituted, for unsupercharged engines up to $2\frac{1}{2}$ litres, so the 1,500 c.c. B.R.M. became a museum piece and they were slow off the mark again with a replacement. This time it was decided to go to the other extreme and use a simple, four-cylinder engine, in marked contrast to the elaborate design of the sixteen-cylinder model.

It was quite obvious that the new 2½ litre, eight-cylinder Mercedes, built regardless of expense on the most advanced lines, as might have been expected from that factory on their return to Grand Prix racing, was going to be the dominant car, as events proved in 1954 and 1955.

IV

It was not until I had raced for a year in the official Mercedes team, with Juan Fangio as the leader, that the B.R.M. story was continued. After a very successful year with the German firm a sensation was caused by the announcement that Mercedes were to withdraw from all forms of racing. No doubt they felt that they had very clearly demonstrated their superiority, and were content to rest on their laurels. After all, motor racing is a very expensive game, and one supposes that they saw no point in spending vast sums when they had nothing to gain and everything to lose. But whatever the policy which dictated the Mercedes decision, it left me high and dry, with no contract signed for 1956.

It was not long, however, before I had a few offers. The B.R.M. was completely new so it conformed with the Grand Prix formula; it was now unsupercharged and, in spite of its past history, it was being persevered with under the sponsorship of the great Owen organisation. I had not entirely lost faith in it, and hoped against hope that trials would prove it to be fit and ready for Grand Prix racing. They called me idealistic, even unrealistic, during that period of trials and tribulations when, in spite of its complete unreliability, I had stood by it. But in fact I was a realist. I wanted more than anything else to win a classic Grand Prix on a British car, and the B.R.M., with its terrific surge of power and its unprecedented acceleration, still seemed to be the only car on which I could realise my ambition.

I felt exactly the same way when I was invited to test the new B.R.M. and, if this proved satisfactory, to drive it in the 1956 series of Grand Prix events. There was nothing I wanted more. I went to Oulton Park for the special tests. The medicine was as before: most impressive in some respects, but still inclined to pack up unexpectedly. It was, undoubtedly, the most difficult G.P. car I have ever handled. We tried loading the front to see if a better distribution of weight would give it greater stability. It did, and no doubt the same result could be obtained by pushing the engine forward a little. But it still seemed to be a potential and not an actual Grand Prix challenger.

Two other British cars were placed at my disposal for testing, with a view to signing up. I tried them both, most assiduously and carefully. The Vanwall, sponsored by Mr. Tony Vandervell, which had achieved a certain amount of distinction in 1955 races, is a superb car to handle, and this was particularly demonstrated on an occasion when I tested the B.R.M., the Vanwall and the Connaught on a slippery Silverstone track. I could get round faster on the Vanwall than on either of the others because it was so steady and so manageable.

The Connaught, which had shocked the Italians by running away with the Syracuse Grand Prix, was just about as fast as the B.R.M. on the wet track; it handled better, but lacked the B.R.M.'s speed. Why the blazes can't we harness that speed to reliability and better handling?

I spent hours and hours thinking and dreaming. Maserati, B.R.M., Vanwall, Connaught; for Maserati had made me a very definite and attractive offer to be their No. 1 driver in all the 1956 races. In my own mind, I was convinced that the Maserati would give me the best chance of becoming the first British driver to win a World's Championship. But, all things being equal, I would much rather drive in British green, or should I say grey-green, because, as I have said before, I am a bit superstitious and don't like an all-green car. That is why I painted my own Maserati in grey and picked it out in green, to comply with necessity.

My mind was almost made up, but always there was that urgent longing to take the wheel of the much criticised, the temperamental, the fickle B.R.M. Maseratis were pressing for a decision, quite naturally. They wanted to tie up their racing programme and choose their team. No doubt the approach to other drivers was contingent on my decision. Then I had an idea. I would seek the advice of experts who also were able to sum up popular opinion, so I asked a party of leading motoring journalists to join me at dinner and, at the Royal Automobile Club, I placed all my cards on the table and more or less invited them to pick out the ace.

There is no doubt at all about the sincerity of those journalist jurymen. They pondered the situation, discussed the pros and cons of placing the title as the keystone of the situation and finally delivered judgment. Of the sixteen motoring scribes who voted, nine were in favour of my joining Maseratis and seven voted for taking a long shot with one of the British cars. That was very even voting, and it didn't do much to help me in making my decision, but it did show that there was a slight bias in favour of my taking what I thought to be my best chance of winning the championship.

One thing I realised and had to consider was that, if I wanted the title, I would have to race against and not with Fangio, who, as the reigning champion, would obviously be No. 1 driver in any team. My contract with Maserati specified that I should be No. 1.

Finally, after a nerve-destroying period of indecision, I accepted the Maserati offer and there, at any rate for the time being, the B.R.M. story ends. But do not be surprised, as I shall not be surprised, if that most fantastic car eventually becomes a world-beater and snatches the chequered flag from the Continental cars.

I bid the B.R.M. farewell, or perhaps *au revoir*, with very great regret, though I cannot really say that I feel any remorse. I am just a professional driver, and, as such, I must stake the strongest claim I can to the quest of the supreme title. But as I drive the Maserati, there will always be with me that haunting snarl of the car which has intrigued me ever since it was first conceived.

The story of the B.R.M. is not a proud one in so far as achievement is concerned, but surely it is a great story in its way, for the great endeavour that has sought to make it a worthy and successful challenger to the supremacy of the Continent. Fickle jade that she is, I still have a high regard for her. Maybe this is not divorce, but just another separation.

No one, I think, foresaw at that time the startling revolution that was to come about in Grand Prix racing over the next few years, when British cars would furnish the majority of the starters with Cooper, Lotus, Vanwall, B.R.M. and Aston Martin, and British and American drivers would be engaged to lead foreign teams.

15

MY BEST YEAR'S RACING

I

AFTER the long lapse in Grand Prix racing on the Continent, there was added interest in the Italian Grand Prix, particularly as the reconstruction of the track and the inclusion of banking made it the fastest circuit in Europe. The new Monza lay-out presented quite a problem, for while smooth track tyres would be more suitable for the flat out banking, they were not suitable for the more normal cornering on the flat. Indeed, the Lancias had so much tyre trouble during practice that they withdrew from the race, much to the dismay of the fervent Italian enthusiasts.

We tried various types of car before deciding on the one best suited to the new conditions, and eventually Fangio and I drove the long wheelbase streamliners which had been specially adapted. The new circuit, or to be more correct, double circuit, measured ten kilometres with the "bowl" offering full-bore motoring. It was on this banking the short chassis Mercedes showed a tendency to lift, so special fairings were fitted so as to trap the air and to hold down the front.

The start of the race saw Fangio, myself and Karl Kling in the first row, and I managed to sneak away with the lead, to hold it over the opening road circuit. Fangio went by on the banking which he took quite low, with myself a little higher, and soon the Mercedes procession led the field, with all four cars, Fangio, Moss, Taruffi and Kling well away from the rest of the field, though the usual challenger, Castellotti, was doing his best to keep us in sight, with Mike Hawthorn on another Ferrari well in the vanguard.

All went well, and according to plan, until the 19th lap, when a stone thrown up by Fangio's car smashed my windscreen. I was in and out of the pits in 1 minute 40 seconds, with a new screen fitted, which was remarkable pit work. To try and catch up I had to do some real motoring, and I managed a couple of laps each in 2 minutes 46·9 seconds for an average of 134·04 m.p.h., and a record for the circuit, but my voyage of recovery was short-lived, for a little later a piston went and I was out of it. Fangio remained at the head of affairs throughout to win at an average of 128·5 m.p.h.

Taruffi (Mercedes) followed him home closely, and then came Castellotti on a Ferrari, which incidentally he had taken over when the Lancias were withdrawn. There were many retirements, but I had some consolation when John Fitch finished on my own Maserati, though he was the last of the nine who completed the race. The Italian Grand Prix settled the World's Championship for Fangio, who could not now be overtaken and there was nobody who could beat me out of second place.

I managed to sandwich a few days' work in after flying back to England, and was then off to Belfast for the historic Tourist Trophy Race, an event dating back from the morning of motoring time. It was the Golden Jubilee of the T.T. and also, as it happened, my birthday. The event was decided over 84 laps of the Dundrod circuit for a total distance of 623 miles. The Mercedes were there in full force, with Fangio and Karl Kling in one car, myself and John Fitch in another and W. von Trips and André Simon in another. The general entry was a magnificent one, with Ferraris, Jaguars, Aston Martins and Maseratis giving battle for the Trophy and a lot of fast but smaller cars out for the Index of Performance Trophy.

Our strongest opposition appeared to be Mike Hawthorn on a works Jaguar, and this proved to be so, though he unluckily blew up in the final stages. Practice showed that my car was wrongly geared, but that was soon put right; there also seemed to be too many cars on the circuit—you notice this particularly when, because you are in one of the fastest ones, you are continually overtaking. It must have been a very thrilling race for the spectators, because the result was in doubt all the way through, but it was also a tragic affair. Early on, there was a pile-up which killed two competitors, but owing to the adequate precautions taken—thanks again to Le Mans—it occurred in a prohibited area from which the public was excluded because it was so obviously a danger-spot.

Since the event counted for the Sports Car Championship it was virtually a scratch race. The start was of the Le Mans type, the drivers dashing across the road to their own cars, parked in echelon. I got away among the leaders and was soon at the head of the field, with Mike Hawthorn chasing me in close company. On the second lap, poor Jim Mayers collided with another car and caught fire at Deer's Leap, and the entire road seemed alight, with great smoke clouds rising. Half a dozen cars were involved in the crashings that followed and they put several drivers out of the race, including Lance Macklin and Ken Wharton.

Steadily, but not very rapidly, I was getting away from Mike and Fangio, but I had to do a little record breaking to do so. On the tenth lap I wasn't too clever at Quarry Corner, and touched the bank without doing any harm. I did not know it at the time, but Fangio, who had started slowly, was coming up fast and for several laps was having a real dog fight with Mike Hawthorn for second place. Indeed, this went on until Mike called into the pits after 25 laps for a routine stop. Then Fangio did likewise and while his car was in the pits, Titterington, local hero who had taken over Mike's car, went by in second place. Then I bought it. My rear right tyre burst while travelling very fast and I snaked up the hill on the far side of the circuit, at about 135, trying to hold the machine on the road. By luck I did this, and came into the pits having lost a little valuable time.

They had to tear part of the wing away before John Fitch could carry on. While my mechanics were sorting things out and adjusting the damaged panelling, Titterington was bringing along the Jaguar at a fast pace and as Fitch drove my car back into the race, he roared by into the lead.

Into third place, behind Fitch, stormed Peter Collins on an Aston Martin. Titterington increased his lead over Fitch and it looked as though the anticipated Mercedes victory was not to be, much to the delight of the crowd, which would have loved to see Titterington and Hawthorn bring home the British Jaguar. Neubauer, seeing the picture change to one which was not at all to his liking, called in Fitch and I took over again. The Jaguar then held a really commanding lead of 3 minutes 23 seconds with Karl Kling second, and myself third. In a little while I passed Kling, and opened up a really exciting chase, in heavy rain, of the flying Jaguar.

At the half distance, Titterington was still ahead but, perceptibly on every lap, I was getting closer and closer. At 50 laps, Mike took over and the pit stop enabled me to get within 25 seconds. Then Fangio replaced Kling and there were the two of us in the silver Mercedes cars giving real battle to Mike and the green Jaguar. At 55 laps I roared by Mike into the lead again, but two laps later I was in the pits for a routine stop and away went Mike passing the stationary Mercedes for a 9 seconds lead. Off again I went and at the end of the next lap was in front again with Mike right on my tail.

Gradually I drew away from him, and so the long, long race drew towards its finish; long for me that is because I had had little rest during the battle. One lap to go and the race "in my pocket" except for any incident on the final circuit. There wasn't one; not for me, but Mike blew up in the last lap but one and so I had won my third Tourist Trophy, with the help of John Fitch. Fangio and

Kling brought home their Mercedes in second place, with von Trips and Simon making it a hat-trick. My average speed was 88·32 m.p.h., but Mike had finally beaten all lap records with a terrific 95·67 m.p.h.

Quite a nice little birthday present, with a new kind of record in that I was now the only man who had won the classic Tourist Trophy Race three times. Obviously the Goddess of Luck was smiling about this time and it was to do so until the end of 1955—my most successful year to date.

II

Following closely on the Tourist Trophy Race came an International Gold Cup Meeting at Oulton. A very impressive field, including Mike Hawthorn on one of the new Lancias—the first time it had raced in England—and Desmond Titterington, whose performance in the T.T. had won for him his first ride in a real Formula 1 car—the Vanwall, the highly spectacular Castellotti (Lancia) and Peter Collins on the B.R.M. and myself on a works Maserati. I already held the record for the course at 85·4 m.p.h., but no fewer than six of us improved on this time during practice.

First on the grid were Mike Hawthorn, myself and Castellotti. Mike and Castellotti went off like bombs at the start, but I was able to head them off in the first lap. The original Lancias were very bad on the road when the tanks were full. Where was the new B.R.M.? Peter had got off to a bad start, but he staggered the crowd with some very fast work which took him from the back of the starting line to third place in four laps, a position in which he stayed until the oil pressure dropped, and the B.R.M. made what had come to be regarded as almost inevitable retirement.

Meanwhile, Mike began dropping back. It was not surprising, for he was a sick man, and nobody can do themselves justice unless they are in tip-top condition. It was, for me, quite an easy race. Having the lead I stayed there, to win quite comfortably at 85·94 m.p.h., with Mike second and Desmond Titterington in the Vanwall winning glory by finishing third in his first Formula 1 race.

I had to leave it to Dad to collect the trophy, for I was due in Germany for a pow-wow with Mercedes, and within a few minutes I was airborne. On to the Riviera for a little recreation. Lots of fun. Out in a boat, a gale sprang up and David Haynes, an amusing friend of mine, and myself were only just able to make harbour. Spear fishing, and I dropped the anchor with the cable unattached, so lost it; saw a Marathon dance, in which the victors kept it up for over 100 hours—ye Gods! Instructions from Germany to proceed to Sicily for the Targa Florio, and caught a plane to Rome, where we did a bit of circling for about an hour because the undercarriage had stuck. Made a good landing and was soon in Sicily, ready for some more racing.

While practising, I developed a touch of 'flu and had a really bad time of it with sleepless nights and a bit of a temperature.

The Targa Florio course is entirely different from any other, a wild, mountainous circuit of just about 40 miles with so many corners and hazards that one must be on the ball the whole time. I spent quite a lot of hours practising and learning the course on several cars before the big race, in which I was to share the driving with Peter Collins in the 300 S.L.R. Mercedes. The course had to be covered 13 times for a full distance of 511 miles, and, because of its inherent danger, it was agreed to start the race at 7 a.m., so that there would be no driving in the dark.

On the morning of the race I felt very little like racing. I had had practically no sleep and was up at 5 a.m., tired and jaded. I felt much better once I was in the cockpit and waiting for the start, and better still when I discovered that I was leading the big field of competitors. Round the tortuous course I sped with the pack howling along behind, the fastest of my pursuers being Castellotti on a Ferrari, with Juan Fangio on his tail. I built up a lead of just over a minute on the first lap, and increased this to five at the end of three laps. Then, wham! I had just come round a right curve and was negotiating a fast left, when I lost control; the car swung its tail out, hit a bank and then bounced off and made straight for a precipice. I was really afraid by now, and tried to bail out, but couldn't. Luckily it turned out to be only a 10 to 12-foot drop and the car landed with a heavy bump. I lost about 12 minutes getting the car on to the road again, and dropped back into fourth place.

Then Peter took over and went like a bomb. Under the rules, no driver was allowed to drive for more than five laps at one time or to take over until his associate driver had accomplished at least three laps. Peter had more than held his own among the leaders, and left me nicely placed when I took over after 8 laps, with another 5 to go. Fangio had held the lead for a brief period, but Peter had beaten him to it and Castellotti was well after him. With the car going superbly, I was able to clip a little off the record in several laps, and so hold on to the lead to the end, to win by 4 minutes 55 seconds from the Fangio–Kling Mercedes which, in turn, was just over 5 minutes up on the Castellotti-Manzon Ferrari. Our race average was 59·79 m.p.h., which may not sound sensational but which, in fact, was two miles an hour faster than the old lap record for the circuit.

Our victory backed by the second car's place, pushing Ferrari into third place, decided the World's Sports Car Championship, for it gave Mercedes a one-point lead over the holders, Ferrari, who had held the lead prior to the Targa Florio.

III

So came the end of that most successful 1955 racing season. There followed a period of T.V. rehearsals, of visits to the

Motor Show, of contemplation of the future and then the rather startling news that Mercedes were going to drop out of racing altogether for 1956. The year had not only brought me some notable victories, but it had taught me a great deal more than I had known about motor racing, especially from my travelling grandstand view of Fangio's technique while chasing him round so many circuits.

My goal was the World's Championship, but with which car should I make my attempt? If only it could be a British car! How I finally made up my mind is told in the chapter dealing with the B.R.M. story, but I can say now, as I said a year ago when I signed the Mercedes contract, my ultimate ambition is to drive a home-built car in the classic events. It is not beyond the prowess of our engineers and our industry to build cars that will give successful challenge to the Continental designers. We have the drivers that could, and do, in fact, match the ability of the Italian and French and German and Argentinian. Not only have we front-rank men of established ability, but the British nursery is full of potential talent. Given the car to win Grand Prix races and championships, we could do it.

It is worthy of consideration that for many years British drivers on British cars have held the world's land speed record.

The final event of the year, the Syracuse Grand Prix, may have been significant. C. A. S. Brooks, certainly the outstanding newcomer of the year, won it on a Connaught. It was his first foreign Grand Prix, but he literally walked away from such men as Musso, Villoresi and Harry Schell, all driving Maseratis, and beat the record for the course as well. It used to be said of our half-hearted enthusiasm for international racing that, even if we had the cars, we hadn't the drivers. But that is not the case today. Continental marques seek British drivers; all we need now are the cars.

Will the Vanwall, Connaught or re-vamped B.R.M. be the answer?

16

I RETURN TO MASERATI

THE year 1956 started rather uncannily with no New Year's Day. This was because I was flying from San Francisco via Honolulu and Fiji to New Zealand, which meant that I lost the day flying over the date line. The year proved to be one of ups and downs, but the World Championship again evaded me and I was runner-up, as in the previous year, to that superb middle-aged meteor, Juan Fangio. It was not that the Maserati lacked speed; it was not a hundred per cent in stamina—an essential for any G.P. race.

As there was a little time to spare before racing started in New Zealand, it gave an opportunity for water ski-ing, a most exhilarating sport. I remember, too, the mild pride I felt at doing a little sewing to fix the British Racing Drivers Club badge on my overalls.

The curtain-raiser, a sports car handicap, provided a comfortable ride and I won on a Porsche open 2-seater. But the Grand Prix which followed was not so pleasant. A good start enabled me to take the lead after the first corner and remain there till the end and win, but it might have been different. With about twenty laps to go the fuel pipe split. This meant the loss of petrol and the necessity of taking on more supplies. There was enough time in hand to take on board another ten gallons, but in the closing stages petrol fumes were so thick that breathing was difficult and no man could have gone on indefinitely. Still it was a promising start to a year's racing.

The bumpy air passage on the way back to San Francisco was a reminder that even air liners do not always have a smooth passage, but the journey saw us crossing the date line again and enjoying two January 8's.

After a few days in Los Angeles I was off on the long flight to Buenos Aires for the Argentine Grand Prix, to meet Fangio, not as a team mate as the previous year, but as a rival.

Practising was not very successful as a piston went in the warming-up process. The mechanics decided to fix the motor after I had done a few laps in a spare car, but I had only won a starting position in the second row behind the first line, Fangio, Castellotti, Musso and Behra. Just to help matters along, the car ran over my foot during race preliminaries, and that was the start of a terrible day. I got away to a good enough start and though the engine did not sound too good I managed to take advantage of other people's casualties and actually was leading after 82 laps. Fangio, having blown up, had taken over Musso's car and he was overhauling me quickly, so was Behra, while my tiring engine began to smoke abominably. Then, in the closing stages the engine failed altogether and Fangio won, to collect valuable points in his defence of the world title. This most disappointing race was followed by the Buenos Aires Sports Car Grand Prix. Better luck came this time with the car running well, except that the brakes were a bit troublesome. Co-driver with me was Carlos Menditeguy, a local driver of well-deserved repute. Juan Fangio tried hard to bring off the double, but while chasing me in second place he blew up and we won quite easily. An interlude at Sebring with Peter Collins in an Aston Martin for the Endurance race was unproductive for we packed up quite early. Then, more flying—I seem to live in the air—back to England in time for cosy little Goodwood.

Here, the opening gambit preceded a rather remarkable sequence of winning races. The Maserati I was driving in the big event managed to beat the record for the track at 96·79 m.p.h. and I won quite easily. This was the race where Mike Hawthorn had rather a narrow escape when his B.R.M. had mechanical troubles and left the road at Fordwater; luckily he got out without much damage.

Next event on the busy calendar was the British Empire Trophy at Oulton, in which my mount was a Cooper, powered by that amazing little Climax engine which has been developed from its original identity as a fire-pump unit. The car did not seem to behave too well in practice, but there was nothing wrong with it during the actual race and although Colin Chapman made a good fight of it, he lost time in a spin and I won at 83·7 m.p.h. which included a record lap. Then we went along to Aintree for the British Automobile Racing Club meeting and this time I won the major event, a 200 mile race for G.P. types, on the Maserati at 84·24 m.p.h.

That event completed the hat trick of consecutive wins on different tracks, Goodwood, Oulton and Aintree, and it was on returning to town from Aintree I had a reminder that there is always a fall after pride. I noticed in a London paper a paragraph under the heading "Moss, Hat Trick". But it was not anything to do with me, it was my namesake! The Middlesex bowler who had taken that day three Gloucestershire wickets in consecutive balls, Rochford, Crapp and Emmett.

That proved to be the end of the run of successes for I failed miserably in the Mille Miglia, that classic road race regarded by many as the most exciting and dangerous of all. If ever an event called for meticulous preparation and practice it is the Mille Miglia, and I certainly practised very thoroughly with Denis Jenkinson, that first-class and most expert passenger/navigator, with whom I had already won the classic race.

It meant early to bed and early to rise, with time checks over the various sections, so there we were, up at the crack of dawn planning and plotting our tactics for the great race but, as a correspondent for a London newspaper told me, the best laid schemes of Moss and men, go awry.

It was a most unpleasant morning for the start, with rain lashing down. Within fifteen minutes we were practically awash and it was difficult to see ahead. It was motoring at its worst, calling for both skill and luck. It did not last too long, however, for on a descent before Rome I braked, locked a front wheel and lost control of the car on the slippery road, and a split second later the car charged a bank, climbed twelve feet, then dropped back to dash across the road. It crashed through a concrete palisade and went over the parapet or embankment, and came to rest just at the edge of a 400-foot drop. It was as close a thing as I ever wish to have.

We managed to get a lift to Rome with an Italian who announced he was in no hurry and was determined to get back; took a train back to Bologna and so back to Brescia, and all we had to show for the Mille Miglia was ignominy and backache! After that it was comforting to win the next big race which was at Silverstone.

The Maserati contract did not preclude me from driving other cars in events in which they were not engaged and it was with delight that I fixed up with Mr. Tony Vandervell to drive a Vanwall, a car of very great promise whose owner had lavished considerable money on research. There is a nice "feel" about the Vanwall; it handles well and it certainly has all the potential for a Grand Prix winner. In practice a very good lap at over 103 m.p.h. opened prospects that augured well, though there was a first-class field for the 180 mile race, including the great Fangio, and Mike Hawthorn on the B.R.M., a car which must surely hold the record for perseverance in adversity. Harry Schell drove the second Vanwall and he had done some fast laps in practice as well. In the race itself Mike Hawthorn went off like a bomb and for 13 laps he had the spectators on their feet, driving superbly to hold on to the lead, with Fangio and myself hot on his tail. Then the apparently inevitable happened and the B.R.M. blew up.

Into the lead I went, with Schell and Fangio in close pursuit, but while the Vanwall took all that was coming to it—and that was plenty—first Schell and then Fangio packed up and I won at the gratifying speed of 100·47 m.p.h. My secret regret was that these winning events did not bring me in any points for the World Championship.

Then came the Monaco Grand Prix—the race of a thousand corners—with World Championship points to be picked up. In practice Fangio had been a split second faster, but in the race itself I was lucky to get to a good start and led from then to the finish. Fangio, giving chase all the time, could not overtake and finished second in Collins' car, with Behra third. The average winning speed of 64·9 m.p.h. may seem a bit slow compared with the Silverstone speeds of over 100 m.p.h., but round the houses at Monte Carlo is an infinitely more precarious business than lapping an aerodrome circuit. Just to show how close success can come to failure was shown about thirty miles from the finish. A competitor just ahead of me braked suddenly on one of the few straights, and I was into him. Almost anything could have happened when I might well have damaged the car, but it picked up immediately and I resumed breathing again!

Racing speeds are determined by the physical limitations of the circuit rather than the power of the engine. To attain good speeds under a variety of track and road conditions it is essential to practice on the course. One must discover the best gear ratios, tyre pressure and carburation settings, and in fact do the best to see the car is tailor-made to the particular circuit on which it is competing.

In short it is a compromise of the capabilities of the car and its adaptability to the course that matters.

The difference in the average speeds in different races—such as at Monaco and Silverstone—is evidence that actual racing speeds have little to do with the speed of which a car is actually capable.

Sandwiched between the Monaco G.P. and further travels on the Continent was a meeting at Crystal Palace, at which I managed to win the Sports Car race and the Formula Libre event in a Cooper and Maserati respectively.

There were lots of classic events ahead of us, and the outcome of the quest for the world title was about this time—in May—quite unpredictable. Jean Behra was top of the form with 10 points, Fangio 9, and myself 8, and Fangio in that position was more than a menace—as he proved to be.

The barometer of good fortune appeared to be set fair at about this time, and since nothing succeeds like success, I looked forward to a good innings. As a change from the sheer out-and-out racers there is the Nurburgring 1,000 kilometre event for sports cars. This is a really gruelling event with about 180 corners per lap, which only takes about ten minutes; it is set in the Eifel Mountains. I shared a Maserati with Jean Behra and there was my old friend Juan Fangio paired up with Eugenio Castellotti on a Ferrari. Peter Collins and Tony Brooks on an Aston Martin represented an all-British combination which did well to finish fifth. A splendid start gave me the road to myself, with Fangio in hot pursuit, but a little later whilst Jean was driving, our car went out with a broken back spring. The pit manager called in the Taruffi car for us to take over, but meanwhile Fangio and Castellotti had collected a lead of nearly four minutes. I chased the Ferrari and managed to knock off some of the leeway so that with four laps to go I was only half a minute behind, but that wanted a lot of picking up when the end was drawing near. But luck came our way when Fangio screamed into the pits for more petrol. The stop, so it was said after, was no more than seventeen seconds, but before he could get his car at peak speed again I had passed him and completed my last lap to win by a little over half a minute at just over 80 m.p.h. I must say that the reception from the German spectators when I crossed the line was very kindly; the previous year I was teamed up with Fangio to drive German Mercedes.

The crowded calendar next brought us to Spa for the Belgian Grand Prix. This is just about the fastest circuit of them all, and with all the top notchers engaged it promised to be an exciting race. I was first away with Castellotti, Peter Collins and Fangio well on my tail. Fangio was all out to rehabilitate himself and win the World Championship and passed me at the end of the Masta straight. He began to draw away though I kept him in sight until, while climbing the long sweeping hill just beyond the pits, one of my rear wheels came adrift, and I had to run back nearly half a mile to the pits. The Maserati pit boys, having seen what happened, flagged in Perdisa on one of the other Maseratis and, within seconds, I was off again on his car. But there was no chance of my getting on terms with the leaders, for Fangio kept breaking the lap record though he was not able to shake off Peter Collins. Towards the close I was signalled to go for the lap record, which meant at least a point in the World Championship. I did it at an average of 124 m.p.h. and it took me into third position, but Fangio, with a lead of 49 seconds, and looking every inch a winner, had the race snatched away from him when his engine failed and let in Peter Collins, and so that brilliant young driver won his first international Grand Prix—and not before time.

The title fight was even more exciting; Collins and myself were level, with Fangio a mere point behind. It was at Spa, that the Vanwall came into the Grand Prix picture, Harry Schell bringing one into fourth place behind me. This so greatly encouraged Mr. Vandervell that he there and then decided to "have a dip" for international honours and began serious research and experiment, so that by 1957 he had a team of Grand Prix racers ready and I signed up to lead a team in what looked like being the strongest challenge to the Continent for many years.

As an interlude before the Rouen Grand Prix meeting, there was the 1,000-kilometre sports car race for the Supercortemaggiore G.P. at Monza. Peter Collins and Mike Hawthorn had teamed up to drive a Ferrari 2-litre in the 620-mile race and they were just invincible, leading from start to finish, with Perdisa and myself bringing the Maserati home in second place about 18 seconds behind: and so to Rouen.

At Rouen I was one of the Aston Martin team, and so was Pete Collins. During practice Peter had put up the fastest time for our team, but on trying his car out I managed to cut off another two seconds, so what did that grand sportsman do but just swopped cars so that I should have the one we believed the faster. I did quite well to finish second behind Castellotti on a 3.5 Ferrari, though I tried my utmost to catch him during the finishing stages, but his car was the faster, and he went over the line four seconds ahead of me.

In spite of the busy time we were having on the race tracks of Europe my thoughts were focused on the British Grand Prix, and I looked forward to Silverstone, not only in the hope of a win but to gather some more championship points.

The position, as far as the world title was concerned before the British Grand Prix, was: Peter Collins 19 points, Jean Behra 14 points, Juan Fangio 13 points, Stirling Moss 12 points. A win meant 8 points, 6 for second, 4 for third, 3 for fourth, 2 for fifth and one for fastest lap.

I had to collect something of this harvest to stand a chance of winning the title. The Maserati had been specially prepared and flown over to England, and when I put in a record lap during practice, doing the three mile circuit in 40·1 secs. for an average of 105 m.p.h., it gave promise, yet actually I did not score a point.

Mike Hawthorn dashed away with the lead and held it for quite a while with me chasing him round. Then Mike dropped out with some sort of lubrication trouble and I was at the head of affairs with Fangio ever ready to deprive me of the lead if given half a chance. Well, it happened. I developed a split fuel tank, and after repeated stops at the pit I had to throw in the sponge due to an axle failure. All I picked up was a meagre point for the fastest lap in the title race. Juan Fangio, in spite of having spun off the track while chasing me, subsequently had matters all his own way and so collected a batch of eight points. Peter Collins was second and Jean Behra third. That meant that the leading three had drawn away from me. Peter Collins scored only three points having shared his car with the Marquis de Portago, but he now led by a single point from Fangio, with Behra third and me still in fourth place, slipping a bit. I was sorry that the Vanwalls had trouble in this event but, after all, you cannot produce Grand Prix cars without teething troubles.

Next really big event was the classical Le Mans, but before then I managed to pick up a win in the Bari Grand Prix in the over 2,000 c.c. class on the 3-litre Maserati.

Favourites for the Le Mans 24-Hour race were the Jaguars which obviously were the fastest of the competing cars and were particularly well manned. At times the race was a nightmare, with torrential rain and a slippery track. There had been special safety precautions to avoid any recurrence of the dreadful disaster that had occurred the previous year, but some of us were not quite satisfied about the safety zone at the pits and the interpretation of the conditions by the officials. The Jaguar team had been entered by the Ecurie Ecosse, and there were one or two other Jags entered by Continental drivers. One of these, Paul Frere, slid off the slippery track quite early in the race, but Mike Hawthorn and Ivor Bueb were well up in front until they lost time with fuel injector trouble. As we roared round the track hour after hour, with Peter Collins and myself taking turns at the wheel, there was plenty of evidence of minor crashes and spills.

In the lead were Ninian Sanderson and Ron Flockhart,

in a Jaguar, and for hour after hour we gave them battle, but our Aston Martin hadn't the power or the speed, and we did pretty well to finish second behind the Jaguar, and not so far behind at that for the winners averaged 104·46 m.p.h. and we clocked 104·04 m.p.h. It was a pleasant and confirmatory victory for British cars, but it was a nightmare of a drive.

Then came another chance for me to improve my position in the World Championship, this being in the German Grand Prix at the Nurburgring. It proved to be a triumph for Juan Fangio, who drove a superb race from beginning to end with nobody to wrest the lead from him. Peter Collins who, like the master, was driving a Ferrari, kept in touch and held the leader in sight for lap after lap till, in the ninth, he stopped at the pits in agony with a fuel leak from which the escaping petrol almost blinded him. The mechanics flagged down de Portago's car and handed over to Pete who made a really heroic effort to get on terms again, but he had a 100 m.p.h. skid and was lucky that the car didn't overturn. He finished in a ditch and was out of the hunt, and it cost him premier position in the championship. It was left to me to hound Fangio round the track and this I did to the best of my ability. We kept beating the lap record while Fangio fought to retain the lead and I fought to take it away from him. But I could make no real impression on the veteran who had taught me so much, and finally he won by a narrow margin at 85·62 m.p.h. and there was the greatest of all drivers back again at the head of affairs in the defence of his title. In fact, it was almost "in the bag", for Collins had only one chance of catching him and that was if he could win the Italian Grand Prix, and get fastest lap, and if Fangio failed to score a point. I had scored six points, but my quest for the title was a hopeless one—Fangio was too far ahead.

The Swedish Grand Prix for sports cars was a dead duck for me, for our car was burned out while refuelling and

Peter Collins was no luckier, for he hit a bank and had to retire, to leave the race to Maurice Trintignant and Ferrari.

I've had some wet rides in my time, but I think the International meeting at Oulton Park gets the aquatic Oscar. It rained torrentially and it took the officials some time to decide that they would hold the meeting. I was engaged in the big race for the *Daily Herald* Trophy, but was persuaded to drive a 1,500 c.c. Cooper in the 1½-litre race for the *Sporting Life* Trophy. I had to start in the third row, but the little Cooper was extremely fast and was soon among the leaders, and then went to the front. Mike Hawthorn had other ideas and kept on my tail in the Lotus. Then he had a really remarkable escape. His car literally leaped into the air and while airborne jumped clean over Salvadori's Cooper. It was a close shave for both of them, the Lotus actually scraping Salvadori's helmet and then crashing into a tree after throwing Mike out. That disposed of the opposition but we were all concerned about Mike's welfare. I hurried along to the hospital tent after winning to discover that he was not badly hurt, though he had to be taken to hospital for X-ray examination.

In the chief race my car was a bit too fast for the opposition and it was just a matter of fighting the rain and the treacherous track. In fact I led from start to finish, but the reporter who described it as a speedboat race had the right phrase.

About this time the racing camps were making overtures to drivers for the 1957 programme, and it is typical of Juan Fangio that he chose this time to say how good the British drivers were. He paid special attention to Peter Collins of whom he said, "he has a very great future in Grand Prix racing," and he also gave it as his opinion that if Moss joined the Vanwall team the Italians would have to look out.

The Italian Grand Prix at Monza was a really exciting event and I think it did a good deal to promote goodwill between us and the Italians, not so much because I won but because of the great sportsmanship of Peter Collins. It started with a breakneck duel between Musso and Castellotti who had apparently set off on a break-up mission, but succeeded only in breaking themselves up. For four laps they ran away from the field; then they both had to come in to change tyres.

Refusing to be drawn into this hell-for-leather business so early in the race I stayed in third place and moved up into premier position when the two leaders came into the pits. Harry Schell on the Vanwall was close behind me and he really demonstrated to the Italians that we had got a crack-a-jack Grand Prix car. Fangio was also only one or two car-lengths away.

Schell took the lead, then Fangio, then myself, then Schell, but eventually Schell had to abandon the race with rear-axle trouble. That gave me quite a fair lead, but Collins and Castellotti were in hot pursuit. The Italian spun off the track and was out of it and then Peter Collins made his noble gesture. Fangio's car was out of it but Collins, who had a chance of winning the world title, handed over to Fangio. Fangio expressed his own astonishment at Pete's action after the race saying "He had a chance of winning the title when he handed over to me." It wasn't all over yet by any means. I set up a lap record on the 47th lap at 135·4 m.p.h., but then had to slow down with the fuel tank dry, and as I crawled to the pits Piotti's car gave me a biff in the back. A moment later Musso shot by in first place. He was going well until dramatically he had to pull in with a flat tyre and his front wheels askew.

By then I was back on the course but pounding along behind me was Fangio and it looked like being a photo-finish. I managed to keep the lead and cross the line less than six seconds ahead of the great Juan who, by finishing second, had successfully defended his world title. There was rather a disconcerting moment when it was stated that Piotti had helped me by that biff in the back. It was suggested that it was a push and there was talk of a protest, but the result stood, and I had won the Italian Grand Prix.

For a while I was able to take things easy and had a thoroughly enjoyable time water ski-ing and generally relaxing before some long flights for my most successful tour ever, embracing the Venezuela Grand Prix, the Australian Grand Prix and the Australian Tourist Trophy, winding up the year with the Nassau Trophy, each of which I managed to win.

What next? Well, I had signed up with Mr. Vandervell to drive Vanwalls in the next year's classics. That elusive world title still is my ambition and I shan't be happy till I get it. Ambition is a pin-point on the horizon and in motor racing, as in most things, you never attain your goal. When hoped-for achievement becomes an established fact you set yourself a more distant goal or a higher target. You may become a master, like Fangio, but you remain a student because there is always something to learn and the only teacher is experience.

Every year I try to become a better driver and I hope it will continue until the essential faculties, among which I count first the rapidity of mental reaction, become dimmed. We are all heading to an unknown ultimate, but it is not only the prowess of the driver which leads us to higher and higher achievement. Equally potent is the development of the car itself. Today we are getting four times the speed of the pioneer Grand Prix drivers, using engines a mere fraction of the size of the monsters with which their cars were equipped.

Every year the driver learns a little more, and so do the designers of the cars. Speeds go up; there is no record which is not at the mercy of improved mechanical and driving efficiency.

That which we regard as phenomenal today will become commonplace; tomorrow's miracle will be the next day's normal.

Almost every long-distance race is a voyage of discovery, which is why we can only strive towards a goal which recedes as we approach it.

I have no thoughts on the potential employment of atomic energy or any other motivator which will take the place of the present orthodox type of engine; I merely wonder where finality begins or progress ends.

Compare the British racer of today with those heroic pioneers who set off on the embryonic cars of yesteryear. They had no attendant crews of mechanics; no expert preparation because experience was being gained. They climbed aboard their blunderbusses, wound up their snorting engines and hiccoughed away over the dusty roads. If they had a puncture they mended the tyre; if their engine faltered, as so often it did, they probably spent the night by the roadside. They had never heard of streamlining; they just drove their vibrating, terrorising juggernauts all out until they reached journey's end or fell by the wayside. Racing garb mostly consisted of warm clothing and strong leather gloves which would, in some measure, insulate the driver's hands against the joggling, vibrating wheel.

Try to visualise those high-built, relatively unsprung cars on which they dashed off at about 50 m.p.h., with their feet treading hard on archaic brakes which did little to arrest their speed while they steered their cumbersome way round the bends.

We are faster, very much faster, but in what relative comfort we drive; how fierce is our acceleration, how potent our brakes; how much easier our gear shifts. So sometimes I wonder what motor racing will be like if I should look back on it as a veteran. Or will motor racing last that long?

The use of inter-com telephony and radar is no longer a matter of conjecture, but can already be practicably and practically applied to motor racing. It won't be long before we have constant contact with our pits. Maybe— horrible thought, we shall have driverless racing cars just as we have pilotless planes.

Under the 2½-litre Formula the trend is always towards lighter and lighter chassis with better brakes and better road holding, assisted by great advances in racing tyre design. In this field, Charles and John Cooper, father and son, and Colin Chapman with his Lotus, were pioneers, the former always adhering to the position of the engine behind the driver. In the classic tradition of front-engined cars, but with a scientifically-studied streamlined body-form, the four-cylinder Vanwall is already as fast and as powerful as the Ferrari, and faster than the 250F Maserati, which is already past the peak of its development.

Looking into the future, we know that the International Sporting Commission, who periodically draw up the new Formula regulations, are as usual anxious about the ever-rising speeds of racing and that it is being whispered that the next Formula to be announced in 1958 for the 1961 season may well be for even smaller engines of only 1,500 c.c., unsupercharged.

Such a step would mean the loss of about 100 brake horse-power, at least in the first year or two. No doubt the delegates of the various nations composing the Commission will thrash the matter out in committee. But the feeling of most designers and drivers in this country is that a 1,500 c.c. Formula 1 would be a backward step. No doubt the racing would be much closer, because, with such limited power and slower cars, more drivers would be able to challenge the top rankers; skill and experience would be, to a great extent, equalized. For instance, corners that now call for real skill with 300 h.p. under the foot, if they are to be taken on the safe limit, would become flat-out, full-throttle curves for almost everybody and there would be a much reduced reserve of power for use in emergencies.

In my view if the very successful 2½-litre Formula must come to an end after its seven-year run a better Formula would admit cars with even bigger engines, up to, say, 3 litres. This would again put ample power into the hands of the drivers most competent to use it, and there are plenty of them today.

The cars would be a little heavier, and safer, with a margin of power suited to the modern technique of cornering on the slide, and the spectacle for those in the grandstands, who, after all, provide the gate-money essential in motor racing, would be even more thrilling than it is today.

INDEX